A Fall From The Top

Matthew & Stacey!

I hope this book

Blesses you

Moray.

A Fall From The Top

My Story
By Moray L.W.H. McGuffie

Published by Gospel One To One

Gospel One To One
Unit 5812
PO Box 92
Cardiff
Wales
CF11 1NB
www.gospelonetoone.co.uk
email: gospelonetoone@gmail.com
Copyright © 2012 by Moray L.W.H. McGuffie and Gospel One To One

Cover design by Moray L.W.H. McGuffie
Book design by Moray L.W.H. McGuffie

First Book Printing: 2012

*"Do not be deceived: God cannot be mocked.
A man reaps what he sows.
The one who sows to please his sinful nature, from
that nature will reap destruction; the one who sows
to please the Spirit, from the Spirit will reap
eternal life."*

Galatians 6: 7-8 (NIV)

*"I thank Christ Jesus our Lord, who has given me
strength, that he considered me faithful, appointing
me to his service. Even though I was once a
blasphemer and a persecutor and a violent man, I
was shown mercy because I acted in ignorance and
unbelief. The grace of our Lord was poured out on
me abundantly, along with the faith and love that
are in Christ Jesus."*

1st Timothy 1: 12-14 (NIV)

Contents

Acknowledgements

I have many people to thank for helping me to produce this book.

First of all, the people who are mentioned in my story. I have made the decision to change the names of a number of them in order to protect their identities. A huge thanks to them all.

Thank you to my wonderful wife Desiree who has always been an encouragement to me all the way through writing the book. She is still my foremost and best critic.

To Jonathan White who helped in the very early stages, as did Sarah Chaplin who encouraged me to think more strategically about what I was writing. Also to Judith Bradley who helped me with the first chapter.

I am very grateful to Evangelists Steve Hill, Tony Anthony and Barry Woodward who all inspired me to begin writing my story after they published their own.

Finally my thanks to Dr Clement Earle, Cath Mogford and Sharon Smith who did the most work of all. I am very much indebted to each of you.

Foreword

Steve Hyde
Senior Pastor of Sedgley Community Church

It's not many times in life that you put down the telephone from speaking to someone for the first time and just know you have made a friend for life. Back in 2007 I spoke to Moray McGuffie about a business proposition and formed a friendship with him that I know was God-ordained. The story you will read in the following pages is just a glimpse of how Moray found a passionate love for Jesus in the midst of some real battles.

The Bible talks about the wise and foolish builders, they were both building, they both faced storms the only difference was the wise man had built his house on solid rock. Moray's story is not unique in the issues he faced and the storms he weathered. What will come through strong and clear from these pages is that he had an encounter with Jesus that gave him the peace and stability he had craved and that money could not buy.

They often say truth is stranger than fiction. Life for many people has twists and turns, and we face head-on situations we never expected to experience. It's amazing how we spend so much time comparing our lives with others around us, often feeling hard done by to and craving someone else's journey. If this story does anything it should dispense with the myth that a man's life is measured by his success or wealth. When Christ is not the centre of your life then all the money, success and influence in the world will give not you the sense of wellbeing you desire.

Life is for living and adventure and success are all part of the God- ordained plan for our lives.

Like the Apostle, Moray has come to the place of being able to say "For me to live is Christ to die is gain". This book is just part of the going story of Moray's adventure with God. The Lord is using him to see many come to Christ and receive physical and spiritual healing. Moray's story is proof once again of God's incredible grace. My prayer as you read this book is that you to will realise that Christ is all you need and that what God has done for Moray he can certainly do for you.

If you are wrestling with life and tying to be someone you are not, stop now! You may not be at the top to fall, you may be at the bottom crawling your way up. Yet wherever you find yourself cry to Jesus - He is all you need.

Colin McKibben
Pastor of the Bridge Church, Neath

I well remember when Moray and I met for the first time. As a family we were in the process of moving from Glasgow to the town of Neath, South Wales to pastor the Bridge Church. On a planned visit to the neighbourhood while looking for schools for our children, my wife Julie told me that we were invited for an evening meal at Moray and his wife Desiree's home by way of welcoming us to the area. I remember asking my wife Julie 'Why are we going, I have never met them before and you barely know Desiree", as they had only briefly met at a women's conference sometime before. Julie's reply to me was "It will be good evening, and I am sure that you will enjoy meeting them. You know I heard that Moray was supposedly a millionaire some years ago?" We went along and had a great evening; we left that night knowing that we had made some really good lifelong friends.

In the subsequent pages of this book Moray goes into detail about many of the important stages and key events of his life. He shares with us some of the stories he remembers from a difficult childhood, of his father, who was a famous musician and composer. He recalls fond memories and some which are not.

You will also learn about the people who were influential to him through the years. Also and importantly the many challenges, difficulties and ups and downs he experienced which ultimately created an extremely focussed and driven person. Someone who aimed to climb to the very top - firstly in martial arts and then the financial services industry, so that he could attain the trappings of wealth that many people would aspire to.

But the story Moray recalls most powerfully is the quite remarkable way that through a chance encounter with a young businessman, he came to meet Jesus Christ and how this has greatly affected his life, his family and indeed his friends.

Moray is one of those people who has boundless energy for sharing the gospel of Jesus Christ. It is his passion, his life; it is always on his mind and on his heart. He just loves serving God and sharing the good news of Jesus Christ.

That has not been the case all his life. It truly is an amazing story.....and it is one that I believe makes good reading.

Introduction

Why did I write this book? Well, simply because it has been on my heart for a number of years. I told my story in a town called Magnolia in Arkansas USA quite a long time ago now and I was asked afterwards if it was available in written form. My answer was "No, but you never know what can happen. Perhaps I will find the time to write it down one day".

Some years later I felt the moment was right. I sat in front of my laptop and started to write about my life. My great hope more than anything else is that by reading this, that you will be able to relate to it and discover the same revelation that I did about who Jesus is, about His life and the sacrificial death He suffered for you and me.

The amazing thing is that Jesus knew the minute, the hour and the day when I would call on His name. Little did I know then how that event would change my life forever and move it in a completely unexpected direction. One thing I have seen many times over the years is that if a person really meets Jesus they will never remain the same.

His timing is completely perfect and I am forever grateful for the Cross of Calvary.

Chapter 1

Can It Get Better Than This?

It was around midnight in 1989 and I was pretty drunk. I had been in Thailand for nearly a week on a free company convention that I had qualified for as a top sales manager. Considering the country and the reputation it had, with Bangkok as a well-known sex capital, it was not surprising that in the main not many men brought their girlfriends or wives on the trip.

I was in the basement nightclub of the Shangri-La Hotel complex, a very large and luxurious site in the country's capital, set on the bank of the River of Kings. That night the music was blaring, with disco lights circling across the room in various psychedelic patterns. There were huge screens on each side of the room with videos playing. I remember Robert Palmer singing on his famous video "Simply Irresistible". The waitresses were all dancing in their tightly fitting black dresses and were all stunningly beautiful. Standing there watching all of this I said to my colleagues "This really is the life".

Over the previous few days I had lost about 48 hours sleep through getting up early to fly to France and then waiting for ages for the main flight to Thailand. I had lain in bed for most of every night with my eyes wide open. Added to that I didn't like the food and as a consequence of missing a few meals the alcohol had gone straight to my head.

The night before my best friend Brian and I had spoken to a couple of the waitresses in the club and had arranged to meet them in central Bangkok the following day. We hailed a Tuk Tuk and arranged to meet them at noon. (A Tuk Tuk is a three- wheeled scooter with a bench seat and a hood so that a few passengers can sit in the back.)

I had only made one excursion out of the hotel, which was to the Red Light district, on the first night of our stay. We returned to the hotel because we simply didn't like it there. We were continually propositioned by men inviting us to clubs, and then of course by an array of prostitutes. Some of these were very attractive and hard for most men to refuse, but we managed to. We were glad because one of our colleagues went off with one of them and found out to his horror that he was in bed with a man! The news of that made us very wary.

On that particular day, the driver who took us into the city pretended that he couldn't understand us. He had obviously duped visitors many times before. "Gullible tourists" he was probably thinking. He took us to a club in a very sleazy and dirty area of the city. We later found out that the drivers would be paid money from the owners of clubs if they brought unsuspecting people to them. When we realised what had happened we climbed out of the Tuk Tuk and had a big argument with the driver.

We were both quite aggressive and were shouting and finger pointing at him for conning us. I noticed out of the corner of my eye that about eight bouncers had come down the steps from the nightclub and were moving quickly towards us. I immediately pointed in their direction and shouted "Brian, look". He turned around and saw them and much to my surprise he marched right up to them all and started pointing and swearing in a very aggressive way.

The bouncers looked puzzled and quickly moved away, back up the steps, to leave him standing there on his own. Prior to working with me Brian was a very highly decorated SBS (Special Boat Squadron) soldier, the Marine version of the SAS (Special Air Service). He had seen plenty of action during his time in the forces. He was the first British soldier to set foot in the Falklands after it was captured by the Argentineans in the early 1980s. I had met and trained with some really hard characters through Martial Arts over the years but Brian had seen action and had killed the enemy. He was very different from anyone I knew. He seemed to fear no one and he certainly wasn't a man to be pushed around.

Eventually, after another Tuk Tuk ride, we met up with the girls as arranged and very quickly realised that we had been tricked a second time. Like the Tuk Tuk driver they had obviously done this before and were very skilled at it. We were taken to buy them gifts and for lunch in a restaurant that the locals ate in. The place was very grubby and dirty which to be honest didn't fill me with much confidence. The dining area was huge and packed with Thai or 'Gooks' as Brian called them. There was a wok with a gas burner directly underneath it in the centre of each round table.

We were taken to sit down and one of the girls said "Would you like meat to eat?" I nodded. She ordered lots of food for us, which was brought out on platters, raw. She tipped all of it into some water along with the vegetables and spices that were in the wok and cooked the mixture in front of us.

She put some food on a plate for me and I popped some meat and noodles into my mouth. The texture of the meat was quite strange, as was the flavour. It was like chewing rubber. After a minute or two I asked, "What sort of meat is this?" She replied "Oh, it is chickens' entrails. You like?" Horrified I said "Chickens' entrails! You mean giblets, the guts?" I was disgusted. I just spat the food out of my mouth. The thought of it still repulses me today. It was yet another reason that I ate only a small amount of the local food during the week that I was there.

With all of that in mind it was no surprise that any alcohol I drank went straight to my head. That evening in the disco, I was very drunk on just a few half bottles of beer. I was in fits of laughter with some of my mates. The waitress who I had taken out that day came over to me and said, "You look vely happy. You vely drunk Yes?" She was around us all the time and not surprisingly, because I had tipped her about six months' wages when she brought us a drink earlier. I had a huge wad of Thai Bart in my pocket. In fact, there was so much of it that I couldn't fold it. I loved the expressions on people's faces when I pulled out the cash to pay for something. I asked the girl how much she earned in a year. The answer she gave was a pitiful amount of just a few thousand Thai Bart. I went into overdrive and boasted that I was earning over 10,000,000 Thai Bart a year. She looked horrified when I told her. I got great pleasure from talking about my income and my success.

At that time I was earning more money than I had ever dreamed was possible. I was now earning on a monthly basis what had been my annual salary in my previous job as a top Cash and Carry manager. I now had Porsches, Jags and BMWs on the drive of my new, luxury home. I had expensive clothes, an array of Savile Row suits for work together with designer shoes. I was a success in most people's eyes, and it meant that I could buy almost anything I wanted.

Life had changed so much for me. I had progressed from being a poor boy from a broken show business family. As a child I had developed into quite a worrier, who was brought up by my mother and two sisters on very little income. Effort, determination and hard work had enabled me to become very accomplished in the Martial Art of karate. I had also risen very quickly up the ladder in my former jobs in retailing and the Cash and Carry industry. In the preceding few years I had discovered something that I was very good at. I could sell, train, motivate, recruit and I had become a real high flier in a large financial services organisation, gaining recognition from my colleagues and bosses, earning a huge salary and building real wealth. I loved my life, my job, and especially myself!

I epitomised the phrase that my colleagues and I used all of the time - "You can if you think you can". I had carefully followed the processes and sales plans that I was taught. This involved goal planning, listening to positive mental attitude tapes and reading the relevant business books. I was totally conditioned to talk the talk and walk the walk. My bosses had taught me to "Think, act, believe and become". I made sure that I followed those words to the letter. My self-esteem was sky high. I was very proud of my achievements and had literally become a 'legend' in my own mind.

I had climbed out of the poverty that I hated and was embarrassed about as a child, to reach these dizzy heights. I was well on my way to the top. Nothing could go wrong now, could it? I mean, could it really get much better than this? Let's face it, I had arrived hadn't I? *I would learn a very powerful lesson over the next few years, that very often, pride comes before a fall.*

Chapter Two

My childhood memories...

I come from a musical showbiz family. Come to think of it even our sewing machine was a Singer! I was born at home in Lambeth, London in July 1957. My parents Jacqueline and Bill already had two daughters, Kathryn and Lorraine.

My father was a Scotsman, who was well known at the time as a Jazz playing pianist and composer, performing on records and the radio and early television.

He worked with many famous bandleaders, musicians and top singers including Frank Sinatra, Nat King Cole and many more. He was also involved in writing music for British radio and later for television shows. These included well-known programmes such as 'Monty Python's Flying Circus' and feature films such as 'Dr Who' with Peter Cushing and 'Too Hot To Handle' with Jayne Mansfield. He also spent time in the USA working on films for MGM Studios. He worked on around fifty films in all and even made brief appearances in a couple of films playing the piano or as an extra.

He was born in 1927 and brought up in Glasgow, where he had an extremely strict upbringing. His mother was very hard on him, especially regarding his piano studies. I remember being told stories of how his mother would whack him on the back of his hands with a ruler when he made mistakes during his piano practice.

As a child he survived falling from an express train, though he was injured. Also during his childhood he caught the second finger of his left hand in the door of a telephone kiosk, the finger turned gangrenous and had to be amputated. However, his missing finger didn't stop him. With great determination and regular practice he became a childhood musical genius, joining the Royal School of Music at a very young age. He played Classical Music, but enjoyed listening to Jazz on records and on the radio.

Once he managed to persuade his father to take him to see a Jazz Concert at a Glasgow theatre. The band turned up to play the gig, but their pianist was unfortunately taken ill. The bandleader came onto the stage apologising, saying that unless there was a pianist in the audience capable of playing, the concert would have to be cancelled. My dad put his hand up. He played the whole gig. He was just fourteen years old and was hooked.

As the years went by my father became very successful and was regularly featured in the national newspapers, especially the Music Press. He became very popular and when he released a record it sold tens of thousands of copies. Later on in his career he won many coveted music awards such as the Ivor Novello Award, as well as being voted the best keyboard player in the New Musical Express on three separate occasions during the 1950s, which was great publicity. Dad was very proud of his achievements and was paid very well indeed.

My mother Jacqueline was born in London in 1928 and when a young girl lived through the bombings of the Second World War. She survived a couple of near misses when many other people died. Her parents were landlords of a large pub where she was raised. It was believed that because the pub was so large it was used as a landmark by the Germans, which meant that it was never bombed! When I was a young boy she told me that she was once riding her bicycle in London when very close by a doodlebug exploded in Regents Park, killing many people. Throughout my childhood she told many stories of the war years which were of great interest to me.

Sometime after the war was over, she was out with friends and met my father while he was playing in a band at a dance.

She was an extremely attractive young woman with the glamour of a film star with long wavy golden blonde hair. Often when people see photographs of her they are amazed by how beautiful she was. Quite definitely a stunner! When my two sisters Kathryn and Lorraine arrived on the scene their births were recorded in national newspapers. The day after I was born a photograph of our whole family was in a number of the national newspapers. One of the headlines of the day was 'Now They Have A Son'.

My earliest memory of my childhood is being wheeled down the stairs in an enormous metal pram with massive wheels and springs, from the large flat where we lived in Brixton, London. We later moved to a house in Raynes Park near Wimbledon, a middle class neighbourhood where I played with the other children from the area in the road even though I was just four years old. Children were generally felt to be quite safe in those times and everyone left their doors unlocked, definitely not like it is today.

When I was a child, celebrities would often come to the house, they were mainly musicians. My mother used to arrange dinner parties, quite often. My sisters and I could hear people singing downstairs and my father playing the piano. The noise would keep us awake so we would occasionally sneak down the stairs to see who was there and what was happening. My father would bark "BED"! We ran up to our rooms quickly as he was not a man with much patience. You did as you were told or you would quickly feel the back of his hand.

There was a talented Jazz singer who visited the house called Danny Street who I liked very much. He always had a smile and a few minutes to talk to me and visited us on a regular basis. He originally trained as a barber and used to cut my hair when I was small.

My father was without doubt a musical genius. He even rivalled many of the top Jazz pianists from America. Just about everyone who knew him liked him a lot. He was considered a success in the music business and being a celebrity meant that he had a lot of hangers-on. Some people genuinely just liked to be around him as he was good company. He was very intelligent and witty and people thought of him as an all round good guy.

I was at a recording studio with him once when I was young. He was part of a band that was playing on a radio play. At the end of the recording session I was introduced to a violinist, who was apparently one of the best in the world. He asked my father to play something for him. He obliged and the violinist stood there and wept as he played.

He sometimes talked about his day at the film studios when he came home. I remember him writing parts as well as taking small roles in the films. One I do recall clearly was 'The Road To Hong Kong', which starred Bing Crosby, Bob Hope and a young Joan Collins. The main composer on the film was Robert Farnon who had a great influence on my Dad's work. When he had to complete a film score he would work day and night for about a week, so that he didn't lose his flow. It was not a good time to disturb him then. No sleep made him very cranky indeed. The music room was always full of tobacco smoke with sheets of hand-written music laid out on the piano and all over the floor.

When I think back to those times I don't have many happy memories of him. He wasn't around much at home because he was working so much. As a result I was often envious of kids who had their fathers at home regularly. There were a few good times. When he was in a good mood he would let me write music on some blank manuscripts. Basically all I could do was to scribble dots and lines on the music staves. When I finished I proudly presented my work to him. He would pretend to play some jumbled up music and we would both end up giggling. One day, completely by accident I wrote a musical phrase. My father used the phrase to write a tune that was actually released on a record, called 'Out Of Cigarettes'. I still have a copy. The photo on the sleeve of the record had a picture of him looking glum next to a cigarette machine that had a sign saying sold out.

Like a lot of musicians at that time he liked alcohol. As was the custom in Scotland he drank whisky and chasers. He became a very heavy and hardened drinker and when he was drunk he used to argue with my mother and beat her. I believe that the beatings my mother took over the years contributed to her becoming dependent on alcohol at times. This made things even worse for her. There were many occasions I remember my mother with black eyes getting me ready for school. She had to walk me there wearing large dark sunglasses even in winter - but they often did not hide the bruises.

My mother wasn't the only one to take a beating though. All of us did especially Kathryn who was the oldest child. When Dad got angry, which was quite often, he hit us so violently that we were hurled from one side of the room to the other. He prodded Kathryn with his finger hard and slapped her when she couldn't recite her alphabet correctly. The constant slaps and prods just made her worse. If I stepped out of line I would get whipped across the backside with the vacuum cleaner power cable. Amazing as it seems, despite all of this very harsh punishment, we still loved him.

I can still vividly recall times when my father was physically abusive to my mother. I watched him smash my mother's head against the wall in our hallway onto a nail sticking out where a picture had once hung and she had to go to hospital for stitches. There was blood everywhere. Another horrible memory of him is when he delivered what was almost a knockout punch to her chin. My mother fell in a heap in a doorway to our kitchen and he then proceeded to slam the sliding door against her legs.

When I was around four years old, my mother became pregnant. Dad denied that the baby was his. One evening he came home and an argument flared up. My mother got a knife from the kitchen drawer and walked around behind him pressing it against her stomach saying that she was going to take her own life. She walked around the house after him shouting, "Admit it is yours or I will kill myself." Eventually she stopped and grabbed a bottle of sleeping pills and emptied them into her mouth. My father just stood there and stared at her. After a while she collapsed on the living room floor in front of me. An ambulance was called and she was rushed to hospital where her stomach was pumped. After all or that she discovered that it was a phantom pregnancy.

Nothing really changed when she came home. The arguments and fights still continued until my father left us for another woman. My mother spent time with a lady friend called Ena who was a very heavy drinker. She could have done without the relationship because it just made our situation worse. It started to affect my schoolwork and attendance. I just didn't want to go there. I would play up, my mother would eventually give in and I did not go to school. After a few weeks the Truant Officer came to our house, which meant I was left with no choice but to attend school. I hated it, especially because I had a very strict teacher called Mrs Lumm. I told the Truant Officer that I really didn't like her. When I returned to her class she pulled me aside and told me that she knew what I had said about her and gave me a hard time about it.

One day my mother spent the afternoon with Ena. She prepared chips for tea and left the chip pan to heat up. Forgetting what she had done the fat overheated and the pan caught fire. The putrid smell of smoke filled the air. In an attempt to clear the smoke she picked the flaming pan up to carry it outside, but tripped as she went through the doorway the winds blew the red hot flames all over her legs. At that time you were not advised to run cold water over a burn. My mother sat in the bathroom with her feet propped up on the bath covered in a blanket. She sat there shaking in agony until the ambulance arrived. She was hospitalised for six weeks while she recovered from the burns so my Dad had to come back home to look after us.

My elder sister Kathryn actually did most of the house work. My father didn't keep his eye on us as he should have and I climbed up a very high wall at the back of our garden and fell. I desperately grabbed at a piece of wood just within my reach that had a large rusty nail sticking out of it, but as I got hold of the wood the nail sunk about three inches into my armpit causing me intense pain. My father rushed me in a taxi to the same hospital where my mother was patient. When we arrived I was screaming in pain making an awful lot of noise. My mother could hear a child that she thought sounded like me from her ward, but no one told her I was there.

My other memory of those weeks was of my father bringing his girlfriend Rosemary to our house, whom none of us liked. He used to make me kiss her and tell her that I loved her. I only did it because I was frightened of him, although as I have already said, I still loved him. I hated Rosemary with a passion! That hatred stayed with me for many years. Dad later married Rosemary.

My father left again when my mother came home from hospital. With him not being around things were very tough indeed. I remember one Christmas day when we had no electricity because he hadn't paid the bill. My mother boiled vegetables in the open fireplace. She lost the grip of the handle as she picked up the saucepan with a tea towel to protect her hands from the heat. This caused her to pour the contents of hot water and Brussel Sprouts all down my back. How I didn't scar I will never know.

When I came home from home from school one day my mother seemed to be unusually happy. She told me that we were going to move to Devon, where her mother lived, so that we could make a fresh start. My father had promised to send money to us a regular basis. My Mum told us that she wanted to open a sewing and knitting shop and to learn how to drive. The thought of us being away from London and the pressure there sounded appealing and the idea of a new life was exciting. However, the day we left I would not go to the toilet on my own at the bus station because I was petrified that my mother would leave me as well!

I wondered whether life would really be better in Devon. I enjoyed looking at the hills and the views on the journey there, which seemed to take ages. It was in 1965 so there weren't many motorways. The first two nights in Devon were spent at a bed and breakfast. After that we lived in bed-sits and even on a holiday caravan site for the summer, which was fun for a while as I made new friends to play with just about every week. My first day at my new school didn't start well. It was called the Blue Coat Primary School for Boys, in Barnstaple, North Devon. I didn't want my mother to leave me there because I was scared that she would disappear altogether. The Headmaster lost patience with me and in the end picked me up and carried me into the school by way of a fireman's lift on his shoulder. I kicked and screamed, shouting "Mummy don't leave me!" I ran away from school every day for a week after that. My mum was well at the time and eventually she convinced me that she wouldn't leave me, so I calmed down and stopped worrying for a while.

I made friends with a boy who was bigger than me and he told me one day in a very strong Devonshire accent that he was the "Bestest fighter in the school". He said "If you gets into any bother with any boys, I will beat them up for you". It was quite comforting to know this, in your first week at a new school. I also made friends with a boy who lived on a cattle farm next to the caravan site where we were living. I used to go over to the farm and spend the day there playing. I was aged seven or eight when one day walking home across the fields a young bull started to trot after me, which scared me. I decided to walk along the road the next time. That is exactly what I did; but the road was a very busy dual carriageway.

After school the next day I walked down the lane towards the major road and that's all I remember. Apparently I had walked out of the opening to be hit by a car that was coming from my right side. My friend said that he heard skidding and a bang and turned around to see me up in the air above the hedge which was at least six feet high. I woke up in a hospital emergency room to see the faces of doctors and nurses staring at me. One of them said, "Look he's coming round." I asked, "Where am I?" My mum was very relieved. The amazing thing is that I didn't break even one bone. I was kept in hospital for a week for check ups and various tests. The good news was that no damage was done. *It is amazing that I wasn't killed.*

The money my father had promised to send never came. That meant no sewing shop and no driving lessons for my mother. In fact one night we were all set to sleep in a bus shelter because we couldn't find anywhere to live. In the early evening my eldest sister Kathryn turned up proudly shaking a set of keys for a bed-sit. She saved the day. In just a few years we moved around a lot, from bed-sit to caravan, to flat, to house, to caravan, to house. Often my mother would get very depressed and would go through some very dark periods. It was very difficult and even now I find it hard to talk about it. The truth is she was ill and very depressed. She really needed some specialist treatment. I loved her very much and it was painful to see her the way she was.

We were walking home from school one afternoon when she told me that her doctor had diagnosed her as having just six months to live. I still don't know what made her tell that lie, but it was probably due to all the beatings and the emotional hurt that had built up over those years. I was frightened for a long time after that and I became a worrier from then. Only my sisters Kathryn and Lorraine got me through that time. I loved them both so much. It was just as difficult for them. Their love and caring was a great help to me.

I continued through junior school though things were tough. The money from my father came on a very irregular basis. Life was okay when mum was well. During these times she was a lot of fun, but when she became depressed life was difficult for us.

We lived in a rented house that had an electricity meter and the landlady called around to empty it on a monthly basis.

Being so short of money my mother devised a plan. Over the course of a few days that involved much trial and error she carefully managed to make a key out of a piece of wire that she used to unlock the padlock on the meter and took the money out. She then put the money back in to the meter so that we could keep the electricity on!

We were poor. All of my friends had bikes, but we just couldn't afford one. I made friends with a boy who was staying with his grandparents for the summer holidays and he rode his bike over to my house to play with me. On the day of his return home he turned up at my house and gave the bike to me. I didn't know what to say. I was just very thankful to him for thinking of me. *My wish had been met.*

At times I used to imagine having money and being a success, but I had no idea how I could attain wealth. It was just a dream for me as it probably is for many people. One thing I recognise is that through all of these tough times the determination to be an achiever of some kind started to develop in me. It came to fruition later in life when I started to experience some success and achievement. I vowed not to be in the same situation as my parents and not to make life difficult for my own children. Someone once asked me what my overriding memory of my childhood was. My answer was "Pain". I was intent avoiding that for my own family.

In her late teens Kathryn met a young man called Martin who was in the army. He was really good match for her. After a while he proposed. Very soon the wedding bells were ringing and she was gone. It all seemed to happen very quickly and left Lorraine and I to support each other.

Chapter 3

At last something to aim for

I only saw my father two or three times in twelve years. I did miss him, but over time I suppose I learned to cope by blocking him out of my mind. The kids in my school knew that my father was famous, and they couldn't work out why we were poor and living in a caravan. I can completely understand their logic now I am older. Classmates often called me a liar when I spoke about him at school, and that did hurt me sometimes. The only occasions I was contacted by him was maybe in a letter to my mother or in a card when he sent money for my birthday and at Christmas.

My mum used to knit my school jumpers, to save money. I hated wearing them because after a while they became baggy and the sleeves would stretch. It was also so embarrassing to say "McGuffie, free dinners" in the school canteen in front of my class mates. The time was a difficult one for me. Children can be cruel sometimes and would say bad things about me and my family. They knew my father was successful, so to see us struggling didn't make sense to them. I hated the fact that we seemed to continually struggle financially.

I started playing the trombone in my first year at Senior School. I had hoped that some of my father's musical ability would be in my genes, but the truth was that I didn't practice playing my instrument as often as I should have. I had a good music teacher called Mr Morgan, who was quite strict. During one lunch break when I was practising in the music room he pulled me to one side. He told me not to keep practising, as he believed that I was wasting my time. I felt under pressure as he was clearly aware of my father's musical prowess and I guess he expected me to be the same. The rebuke from my teacher had a positive effect on me. Having to hand back my trombone would have caused me great embarrassment, considering my father's successful career. I started practising regularly which I was aware I should have been doing. I practised at home, at break times and at lunch times, which helped me to improve considerably over a short period of time. The effort paid off as within just a few months I was playing in the local orchestra, which met twice a week in the evenings for practice at the school.

We performed at lots of concerts, which I enjoyed very much. Playing an instrument meant that I also did well in Music, getting grade A on my school report. After a year or so I was promoted to First Trombone and regularly performed solos at concerts, which always went well. My music teacher had a mastery of most of the brass instruments but I was soon better than he was. Hard work, concentration and the blocking out of any distractions became traits that I developed over the years. I am now grateful to Mr Morgan for giving me that push.

I excelled in the French lessons. For some reason I was able to pick it up very quickly. I watched a television series at home with my mother on Sunday mornings called "Repondez S'il Vous Plait" which was a French course for adults. That year I became the top student in my group. I was able to converse in French very well, getting the correct accent came very easily to me and by the end of my studies I was very nearly fluent. My French teachers used to make me sit in with the students who were three years ahead of me. I was proud of the fact that I could converse better than anyone else my age could.

I also excelled in Sports. I desperately wanted to be in the school football team but didn't quite make the grade, which was a disappointment. I really loved football and still do to this day, especially Manchester United with my heroes of the time being George Best, Bobby Charlton and Denis Law. I watched them win the European cup in 1968 and was hooked. I used to play the football game called Subbuteo on my own and with friends. The green pitch was laid out on my bedroom floor. Though I'd be playing upstairs in my room, I could often be heard downstairs! My mother and sisters would hear me commentating on every move I made during the game, shouting things like, "Charlton passes to Law to Best, he shoots and scores, Yesss!" Although I was an asthmatic, I enjoyed any physical activity and joined the Gymnastics class, which was an after school club, often taking part in the various Gymnastics demonstrations that were held.

The physical training helped me a lot later in life. I used to run just about everywhere! As a result of this I became one of the best long distance runners in the school. One year I ran in a three-mile road race. The course was along quiet lanes and across fields and I actually walked part of it. I was very surprised when a teacher told me that I was in sixth place. Annoyed with myself, I realised that I could have covered the distance far quicker with just a little more effort.

The subjects that I found great fun were English and Drama. I loved acting and performed in every school play. I took lead roles in my last three years there. We often did Improvised drama which was especially enjoyable. I loved the challenge of it and was thrilled when the audience laughed.

When I was fourteen I started mixing with a group of older boys who had already left school and began under-age drinking and going out with girls. These boys became good friends. Everyone had a nickname except me - Shutey, Speedy, Boney (because he was so skinny) and Guzzi. They were all at least a couple of years older than me. I started staying out till late which caused my schoolwork to suffer. I became rebellious in class and was often in trouble with the teachers. On one occasion for misbehaviour in a lesson I lost a credit mark for my entire class in a school competition. We ended up losing by just one point! Nearly all the boys from my class waited for me after school and gave me a beating.

Occasionally I got into tricky situations with some of the tougher lads. I would be afraid, but would usually be able to get free by either telling jokes, acting the fool or by simply by using the proven last resort of running away! Unfortunately I wasn't always successful and got knocked around a few times over the years.

During my last school years which was the early 1970s skinheads and the suede heads (who were slightly more fashionable and could have longer hair in a feather cut style) became the big thing and were talked about in all the classrooms. I really wanted to be tough like some of the kids that dressed that way in my class. The problem was that we couldn't afford the clothes, so I didn't even have the chance to look like one! Those boys whose parents bought them the trendy clothes gained respect from the other kids in school. I desperately wanted that respect. We were still poor in relation to most of the other families in the area. Looking back I can see there was a huge void in my life due to all the problems with my mother having many emotional scars and depression and the absence of my father. I wanted to be popular in some way - I wanted to be like other people and accepted by them. In school the footballers, the skinheads and families with money always seemed to be the most popular.

Other children would see my Dad on TV or perhaps hear him on the radio, and then see that I had free school dinners and it didn't make sense to them. The main way I got recognition was by being the class jester. Cracking jokes and clowning around used to make people laugh including my teachers. I used to do impressions of them and perform little sketches that I devised. I am still like it today and somehow I am able to remember a huge amount of funny stories to use as ice breakers when I meet people for the first time.

During a lunch break my French teacher Mr Kanean, who I respected, caught me misbehaving in a school corridor. He made me march backwards past groups of smiling children and teachers, in fact almost through the entire school asking continually me in a loud voice "Why are you walking backwards McGuffie?" My reply to each question was "I don't know Sir". When we eventually got to his classroom he said, "I will tell you why you were walking backwards McGuffie, it's because you are a backward pupil!" He then said something that I have never forgotten and I have repeated it many times to my children. He asked me "Do you know what you are going to be when you grow up?" "No Sir!" I replied. He then said with a very austere tone, "You are going to be an 'I wish I'd', McGuffie'. I asked, "What does that mean sir?" He sternly replied "You'll say to yourself when you are older 'I wish I'd worked harder when I was at school'". He was right; I genuinely regret that I didn't work harder during my time at school.

In my final year the army came to the school on a recruitment drive. I was about 5'3" and quite puny. A lad in my class called John Huxtable who didn't like me that much, asked me to box with him as the army was doing boxing training which would end in some fights. In order to gain acceptance I agreed. However, there was a problem that I hadn't taken into consideration regarding my opponent - he was like a giant compared to me! In the days running up to the event I practiced boxing alone in my bedroom, trying to remember techniques used by the boxers I had watched on television, like Henry Cooper and Mohamed Ali. I convinced myself that if I mirrored what they did, it would give me a better chance.

After a bit of training the matches were organised. We told the instructor we wanted to box each other. He looked up at John and then down at me and said "Okay" looking at me with an "Are you really sure that you what you are doing?" expression on his face. We were put together in a make shift ring wearing huge boxing gloves. The instructor shouted, "Start boxing!" I began reasonably well throwing out a few punches to keep him away. I am sure you won't be surprised to learn that I was soundly beaten.

John avoided my weak jabs and before I knew it he was all over me, pounding his fists into my stomach and face. He was giving me a real hiding. We broke and he waved his fist in the air to his friends. A voice from the crowd called out "John!" He turned his head to see who it was; just as I was throwing my best right handed punch. Smack! It nearly knocked him over and made him stagger back a few paces. There was a roar from the spectators. Unfortunately for me though, he regained his balance and threw a flurry of punches into my face! After a couple of minutes the army trainer had to stop the fight because I was not conscious of what was going on. It wasn't just my body that was hurt but my pride also. My plan to be accepted as one of the lads had failed miserably.

My memory of childhood is that we were always short of money. One Christmas time we had no money for food and the situation was getting desperate. My mother had been waiting for a cheque for £10 all of the week leading up to Christmas. No post arrived, even on Christmas Eve morning. I went with my mother to the shops to spend the few pennies she had. We got home to find that the cheque had arrived in the second post. We ran to the Post Office to cash it and then to the supermarket for food and Christmas Crackers.

When I left school at the age of fifteen I had just five CSE qualifications. Mr Kanean had been correct; I did indeed wish that I had worked harder while at school, knowing that I could have done much better. I managed to get a full time job straight away and started working in a local supermarket in trainee management. The store manager offered me a position because he had noticed that I had been doing a good job working there on Friday evenings and Saturdays.

However, I joked around quite a bit and was often in trouble with my bosses for that and for not working when I should have been. When I concentrated, I did a good job and got a lot of satisfaction from it. I had a talent for shop work, but was somewhat inconsistent. I really enjoyed dealing with customers, laughing and joking with them, building up a rapport.

One day I was asked to sweep up at the front of the store. A lad who was a local skinhead was standing outside with a few girls. He was a year younger than me. He started showing off to his friends, acting like a tough guy and mocking me. I told him to shut up. He became very angry and challenged me to a fight. To my great relief, I was called back into the shop by the branch manager. I made sure to avoid the boy like the plague after that episode. Deep down though, I desperately wanted to be like him, to be shown some respect by the lads and girls in the area being regarded as a tough guy.

At the supermarket there was a boy working as a trainee butcher who had been in the same class as me at school. He was a lot bigger than me and used to badger me all the time in the staff canteen, at tea and dinner breaks. He did this for weeks. I began to hate him and used to imagine myself beating him up, blow-by-blow, kick-by-kick, leaving him in a bloodied pile. I rehearsed it in my mind over and over again. One day he went too far, so I decided that the next time he provoked me I would retaliate. Enough was enough.

It didn't take long as he started verbally abusing me the very next break time. I stood up and told him to shut his mouth or step outside because I wasn't taking any more of his comments. The canteen was mainly full of women. There was complete silence as everyone waited to see what happened next. He looked really shocked and backed down. He never bothered me in any way again. The incident did a lot for my self-esteem and confidence.

When I was fifteen I loved watching the television programme called 'Kung Fu'. I used to try to do the moves like Kwai Chang Kane and perform the techniques that I saw in the programme. In all truth I was terrible at it. I often imagined myself beating up people like he did. Around that time there was a new Kung Fu film released at the cinema called 'Enter the Dragon' starring the late Bruce Lee. There was an advert on television and a feature on a television programme called 'Pebble Mill at One'. I decided to go and see it with a lad my age from work.

To get into the cinema we lied at the ticket booth about our ages saying that we were both eighteen. I sat in the cinema seat completely mesmerised by what was happening on the screen in front of me. I knew in those moments that I wanted to learn this type of fighting system, hoping it would build my confidence even further, my reasoning being that people in the area would respect me because of it and would more readily accept me.

It was amazing how this little guy was beating up lots of people. After seeing the film ten times over the next couple of months, I decided that I wanted to be like the Kung Fu fighter and searched around for a Kung Fu club.

Unfortunately there weren't any nearby. There was a Shotokan Karate club though, so I decided to go along and take a look.

The classes were at a school hall. Having persuaded a friend to go with me, we watched together though a window. Impressed by what I saw I joined the club and started training with a brilliant instructor called Gibson Towns who was a Brown Belt (two grades away from Black Belt) at that time. He was very strict and pushed all his students very hard indeed.

The Karate colour belt system worked in this way:

White Belt in 10 Novice
White with a red stripe in 9th kyu
White with two red stripes in 8th kyu
Yellow in 7th kyu
Green in 6th kyu
Purple in 5th kyu
Purple and white in 4th kyu
Brown in 3rd and 2nd kyu
Brown and white in 1st kyu
Finishing with the coveted Black or Dan 1-10 (they go from 1 to 12, 1st, 2nd etc.)

There were about thirty people in the class when I joined. Learning the techniques was complicated, but very enjoyable. It was extremely physical and tough. I often went home with bruises and over the years I got injured several times. We used to do stomach punching and body-conditioning exercises. We always did a lot of fighting. My previous Gymnastic ability helped me considerably and very quickly I realised that I was better than many of the people I trained with which caused my confidence to grow considerably more. I demonstrated these new skills to my friends who were impressed. Soon the news got around that I was learning Karate and opinions of me began to change.

At this time my sister Lorraine left home to get married. She has since said that she will never forget the expression on my face when she broke the news that she was leaving home. Not long after that I moved out to a friend's house because I was finding it very hard at home with my mother as she was going through another battle with depression. We shared the cost of the rent but the place was so dirty that I only stayed there for a couple of weeks. I returned home with nowhere else to go.

A short time afterwards, my mother said we were going to move in with a man she had befriended. It was fine for a while but I soon realised that I didn't like him and the feeling was mutual. He was irritated by my Karate moves as I was often kicking and punching around the house. Knowing that he disliked me doing it made me do it even more! I could kick so quickly that my trousers made a very loud cracking noise rather like a whip. The house was around the corner from my girlfriend's, which was convenient. My mum went out most nights for a drink with her new man. They started to argue often, which made things very awkward, and which brought a very uncomfortable atmosphere to the home.

Through Karate my self-esteem and confidence continued to grow. I was getting fitter, stronger and leaner. My kicks and punches became faster and more powerful. I had left the supermarket and was working in a furniture store as a salesman. I used to go upstairs in the store and punch and kick the rolls of carpet when no one was around. Once I found a huge roll of brown paper that stood about six feet tall. I could just about manage to get my arms around it to move it, as it was extremely heavy. I decided that I would try out a technique I had recently learned, called a 'Spinning Back Thrust Kick'. (This is a powerful kick where you turn your back towards an opponent and drive out your leg with great force.) Hoping that I would be able to knock it over onto the floor, I stood before it in a free-style fighting posture composing myself, ready to attack. I spun round and thrust my right leg out with full power and hit the roll right in the middle, Kiahing (shouting loudly with fighting spirit) "Eeeyaaahh!!!" I was amazed to watch the heavy roll completely lift off the floor and fly across the room horizontally into a glass coffee table, smashing it into pieces. I got into a lot of trouble and of course had to pay for the damage, which was about a week's wages!

All the training I had been doing was building up my body, enabling me to deliver karate techniques with great speed, force and power. On a night out with some friends, having had too much alcohol I offered to help a friend who had put some money in a bubble gum machine fitted to a wall outside of a news agents. His coin had become stuck in the mechanism which meant his gum would not be dispensed. I asked him to stand aside while I struck the side of it with the heel of my hand. I expected to hear the coin drop as I made contact, but the force of the technique ripped the machine right off the wall making it smash onto the floor. Glass and bubble gum was all over the pavement. We made a quick getaway before the police arrived. The noise made quite a disturbance.

Whilst training one evening, I was sparring with a student who was at least a foot taller than me. I made a fairly poor attempt to block a powerful kick. I felt a very sharp jabbing pain in my arm. I went over to my instructor who just shook it. All that did was to make it hurt even more. An x-ray revealed a fractured bone which meant I went home with my arm in plaster. I had to have six weeks off work and as a result I lost my job.

I trained at home almost every day, practising stances, kicks and stretching exercises. My legs grew much stronger and my flexibility increased. On the day the plaster removed, I went straight back to the Karate class and was very sharp indeed. My kicking techniques were far superior to those of my fellow ungraded students, as well as many of those who were ranked above me.

One morning my mother told me that she had found a diary where we were living, that was written by her boyfriend. She said that it was disgusting, perverted, that the entries in it were obscene. Their arguments became more frequent after this and there were often periods when they wouldn't speak to each other.

Chapter 4

Confidence Building

My family did not go to church. Christianity was hardly ever discussed and I knew very little about God. The truth was that I found all that type of thing very boring. I didn't particularly like Christians for some reason, I don't know why. I had heard from my mother that God was supposed to be everywhere around us, but I didn't understand that at all. At school we sang songs about God and His Son Jesus and we performed the Nativity Play just before the Christmas break. I watched the occasional Christian film during the Christmas holiday and at Easter-time but that was about it. I don't remember having a Bible in our home. When we lived in London we had a book by the Evangelist Billy Graham, but it was only when I was in my forties that I discovered our family's very strong Christian heritage with a good part of my Scottish family being committed, born again Christians.

When I was young some Mormons called on us but they did not get a warm welcome. I went to church for the couple of weeks before my sister Kathryn got married. Other than that I had no knowledge about anything connected with religion and I had no desire to know more. The few churches I had attended seemed to be dead to me, with absolutely no atmosphere. Once on a TV programme I saw some Christians singing and holding their hands in the air as they sang. I laughed to myself and thought that they were freaks.

After weeks of arguments with her boyfriend my mother and I were both told to leave the house. She went to stay with her mother and I moved in with my girlfriend at her parent's house. I had to make a decision on what to do next; we had been dating for a while. We got engaged when we were both seventeen and initially made no firm plans for a wedding. However, despite being far too young we were pushed into getting married. We planned for the wedding to take place in three months. We were both just eighteen at the time.

I found a second floor flat in Barnstaple for £8.50 a month and moved in on my own until the wedding day. I remember the service was boring. The vicar, who was known locally as a drinker, conducted it. It gave me more reason to a have a bad opinion of what Christians were like, "Hypocrites" I thought. Well, it made sense to me anyway. I gave a very mumbled speech at the wedding reception that lasted for about thirty seconds! I was absolutely petrified and could never have imagined then that the time would come when would be speaking publically with confidence.

I continued with my Karate training and now held the grade Yellow Belt, having passed 3 grading examinations. I was offered the opportunity to go to a week-long training course for at Crystal Palace in London sponsored by a wealthy businessman. It was my first chance to be trained by Japanese instructors. I had heard stories, read about them and couldn't wait to get there! The most exciting prospect was that I would not only train with top instructors but also the legendary Kienosuke Enoeda who at the time was ranked at seventh Dan (Seventh Degree Black Belt). All the Japanese instructors were fantastic but Sensei (teacher)

Enoeda was something else! He was so powerful and his technique was outstanding. He and the other instructors, in particular Tomita Sensei, made a very big impression on me. I learned a tremendous amount on the course and was awarded Green Belt after taking a grading examination at the end of the week.

I was now working at a local independent discount supermarket, owned by a well-known businessman, Brian Ford. Before I got married I would often be in trouble with the manager for messing around. He was a Christian man called John Holland, a very honest and good person, but he had to pull me aside a few times to reprimand me for slacking and being quite lazy at times. I was lucky to stay in the job to be completely honest! On my return from my honeymoon I was moved into the warehouse for a couple of weeks. It was enjoyable there; busy all the time and my co-workers were fun to work with. One morning the manager called me aside. I thought it was for another telling off. He said "Moray, I want you to know that Mr. Ford and I have been keeping an eye on you for the last few weeks". "Oh no!" I thought. He continued "I want you to know that we are very impressed indeed. Keep up the good work and you will be given more responsibility. The ball is in your court." I was stunned, realising that more responsibility meant more money. I was earning £19 a week so decided to get my head down work hard and see what the outcome would be. As I look back, I realise that the short meeting with Mr Holland was a pivotal moment in my life and from that time, things dramatically improved.

My wife and I were newlyweds. It was fine for a few weeks, but our arguments soon began. They frequently ended with her taking off her wedding ring and threatening to leave. This happened regularly, becoming the norm over the next fifteen years. I probably caused many of the rows and they were not all her fault. We simply hadn't married for the right reasons; our frequent arguments were an inevitable result of that.

We didn't like the flat we were living in but were not earning enough to save for a deposit to buy a house. I decided to really go for it at work. After some hard thinking, I came up with a plan to get my head down, roll my sleeves up and work very hard. I started work five minutes before everyone else; ensured that I was the last in and first out of every break and always worked for five or ten minutes longer than anyone else. After a month or so, Mr Holland called me to his office. This time it was different because he told me that he was going to give me a promotion and a higher wage.

I continued to work hard and within twelve months was promoted three times, now earning £40 a week. The extra effort meant that my salary had more than doubled in that time and my self confidence grew too, as my boss even let me run the store on my own at weekends. It felt great to wear a jacket and a tie instead of the normal store overalls. It gave me even more confidence in my abilities and myself. Extra effort reaped rewards both in my job and in my Karate training.

My headmaster used to say in school assemblies, "The more you put in, the more you will get out". He was certainly right and what I had been doing was proof of that. Now more confident, fitter, stronger, knowing I could handle myself in a fight; I was now teaching at the Karate club and the captain of the clubs Karate team. At work I was a senior manager and had the respect of my bosses, the business owner and the people I was working with. Receiving recognition within the karate club and at work gave me great satisfaction.

A significant change had taken place in my mindset; I had stopped worrying about what other people thought of me. I genuinely believed that if I applied myself, I could do anything. I had come a long way in just a few years; from an insecure wimp to believing that the world was my oyster. My attitude had changed dramatically; having confidence in myself at last was exhilarating.

I went to see Mr Holland one day to ask for advice about getting a mortgage to buy a house. He sent my wife and me for an appointment at a local building society because he knew the manager. We were offered a mortgage but it was not enough to buy the house we wanted, which was for sale at £7,000. The next day at work, he asked how we'd got on. We had been offered a loan but it wasn't quite enough, so that meant saving up for a larger deposit. Later that day I was called to the owner's office where Mr Ford told me that he had phoned the building society manager and asked how much extra a year I would need to earn to get the mortgage. He gave me a twelve percent pay rise there and then and we moved into the house a few weeks later.

My Karate continued to improve and I had progressed though two Purple Belts and three Brown Belts. The training was tough because we were being continually pushed. My physique changed, as my muscles became stronger. The

Karate moves were delivered with much greater speed, power and accuracy. My reactions were improving through fighting at every lesson with different students.

In all the years of doing Karate we never got into the spiritual side of it. We treated it purely as sport, though some people who told me that they had some weird experiences. A few even said that they could watch themselves fighting from the other side of the room. I thought that they were off their heads and didn't have any desire to get into anything like that. My aim was simply to be fit and strong.

Over a five year period, due to the very tough training regime, everyone who was a higher graded belt above me when I had begun had by then left the club. It meant that I was the highest graded there along with just one other student. My instructor Gibi asked if I wanted to attempt the Black Belt examination. I said that I certainly did, more than anything else. He replied, "Well if you think that the training has been hard to get to where you are now, you are in for a surprise, it is going to be much tougher!"

He was absolutely right; it seemed like he beat me up at every lesson for the next six months! The hard training, the bruises and the beatings I took over that period were just a process I had to go through to reach my goal. I told myself "No pain, no gain" and was totally focussed on achieving that ultimate goal, the Black Belt grading. I would do all I possibly could to attain it.

Chapter 5

Push Push Push!

My job was going very well and I was now effectively the deputy manager. I had reached the highest level I could in the company and spent a lot of time with Mr Holland learning and training. We worked on ideas that could develop the business further, including store layouts, pricing, promotions and customer incentives. He taught me a tremendous amount regarding the day-to-day running of the store, which I have never forgotten, including how to manage the staff effectively. We covered areas like planning and prioritising to get tasks done efficiently. It was excellent grounding for my future career. The company also put me forward for management courses to study at home, which increased my knowledge much further.

At the same time though, because of the success I had experienced and I was finding myself in a bottleneck career wise, I started to get a bit restless and considered looking for another job. I applied for a job in the Police Force and passed the entrance exam for a number of constabularies but not for Avon and Somerset, the one I particularly wanted to join. I had the flu at the time and wasn't in the right frame of mind for exams to say the very least! Mr Kanean's words telling me that I'd "wish I had worked harder when at school" rang in my ears when I was given my results by the examiner. It was a painful lesson.

In the New Year of 1978 I read a newspaper article about horoscopes. Like many people, I always used to read them at the start of the year. My horoscope was for a 'champagne year' - a year of success. The fact that there were about six million people in the UK plus many millions more worldwide with my birth sign didn't cross my mind! Did that mean it was going to be everyone's year of success, or just those that read the newspaper? There were some successes and some disappointments throughout the year, but from then on I started to read the horoscopes daily hoping to find some good news and I suppose some hope and inspiration for the future. *I now know I was looking in the wrong place entirely.*

As he had forewarned, the training with Gibi got steadily harder and more intense. In addition to his training I practised a great deal alone, running, exercises, stretching, I practiced kicking, punching and blocking routines; a set fight sequences with imaginary opponents, (called Kata). Over a six month period, I must have practised my grading examination kata called Bassai Dai (To penetrate a fortress) hundreds of times, perfecting a smoother and more powerful performance. I ensured that my stances were always strong, low and correct, moving my head and eyes towards imaginary assailants before they attacked. When practicing kata it is necessary to put in the same effort as if it was a real fight with several opponents and to demonstrate tremendous fighting spirit. On completion of the exercise you should be as worn out as if you had done it for real. I used to practice this and other regimes at the back of the Cash and Carry almost every day.

I was eating a massive amount at the time as well, yet I only weighed ten and a half stones. In fact all I seemed to do was eat, but I was burning off all of the calories and fat content with all of the practice and exercise. Push, push, push.

The pace of the practice with Gibi increased even more dramatically over the month leading up to the final session before going to Crystal Palace for my grading. I dreaded this last practice with him, as I knew that the session was going to be a painful one for me. It would involve what we called fighting spirit training, which involved being pushed to what felt like complete exhaustion - and then being pushed even further!

I seriously considered quitting that evening, as it was so incredibly hard. During the training a thought went through my mind "Shall I say I am going to be sick, so that I can get out of this?" Then I thought, "When I fight again tonight shall I exaggerate a kick to my stomach and collapse on the floor so I will have a chance to recover?" However, what I had been taught was "Never give in, never give up" Gibi did not tolerate any kind of slacking or bad attitude. He told me once that it was not just about passing my Black Belt; it was about holding my grade. I had to be an example to the students, possessing better fighting spirit, better technique and a better attitude. He reprimanded me once when I didn't bow properly to a lower grade. He was extremely strict, but always got the best out of his students.

I kept telling myself, "Come on you can do it! Not much longer now! He just wants to see the fire in your eyes! He wants to see you push on in the face of adversity! Show him your fighting spirit! He's doing this because he doesn't want you to fail! Keep on going, not much longer, it will be over soon!" He pushed us both so hard that night that it was bordering on agony. I remember looking at myself in the mirror after the session. I had a very fat lip, a bloody nose, red punch and kick marks all over my face and body. I wondered if it was worth all of the pain. The answer to that would come the following week at the grading examination.

My colleagues at work wished me all the best for the course. I left my wife at home and travelled to London with a few other students from our club. I was both excited and very apprehensive when I arrived at Crystal Palace for the five-day training course. Around five hundred students of all grades from all over the world attended. I trained with over one hundred Brown Belts. Each day consisted of two sessions and each with a different Japanese instructor, making the training both varied and very demanding. Friday was for a pre-grading session followed by the actual examination in the afternoon with over thirty people attempting Shodan (1st Dan Black Belt). I was so nervous during the lunch break that I couldn't eat a thing. My stomach was in a knot and churning. Before the grading examination started Gibi encouraged me by saying that the last training evening I had at our Dojo (Training hall) was a lot harder than this was going to be. He knew I could do it and he told me that he believed in me.

Having taken grades under the Japanese before, it was normal for an English speaker to call out a person's name, especially with an unusual surname like mine. However, Sensei Enoeda read mine out perfectly. I was startled by it and quickly stood to my feet and shouted "Oss Sensei!" My mouth went completely dry. He called me over to the desk and lectured me because I hadn't updated my address on my grading application which was incorrect since I had recently moved house. He was really angry and shook my licence at me as he spoke. I apologised, continually bowing and saying that it was an oversight on my part. He angrily motioned me away to sit down on the floor. I was very concerned because he seemed to be so irritated by my mistake.

The first two parts of the grading went well which involved demonstrating various techniques moving from one side of the sports hall to the other. The last part of the examination was free fighting. I was sitting next to a guy who also trained at our club. He was a few years older than me, a biker and looked like a Hells Angel with his long brown hair, long beard and tattoos. He said to me with a very mean expression on his face "Look, if we get called out to fight together, don't you give a quarter, because I'm not going to". "Neither will I!" was my reply. There were thirty-three of us sat there, the names were drawn out of a hat and we were both called out together. We bowed then stood ready in a free fighting stance waiting for the command to commence fighting. Enoeda Sensei shouted "Ashume!" (Begin).

We immediately started fighting hard and fast. We had fought each other many times over the years so we knew each other well and the match was very even. We managed to either evade or defend each other's attacks. My opponent started to aim front snap kicks at my stomach area; he was keeping the weight on his back leg for balance. I defended these three or four times. The next kick came, I padded it down, while his kicking foot was barely on the ground, then I stormed in with a Foot Sweep on his supporting leg with my right foot, which lifted him into the air to where he was face height and horizontal. I followed up with a powerful lunging, jabbing punch (Kizami Tsuki) to his face making a loud and ferocious roar Yeeeaarrgh!! My fist slammed into face while he seemed to hang in mid air, Smack! He bounced off my punch like a ball off a bat and fell straight on the floor in front of where Sensei Enoeda was sitting! He looked straight at me, "Control!" he shouted. "Sorry Sensei!" I replied. Other than a little lack of control the technique would have won any competition fight, because it was a full point scoring punch. We continued to fight on for a couple of minutes and were then sent back to wait for the remainder of the students to fight each other. I looked up to see Enoeda Sensei holding my licence in his hand as he pointed to me. He was still very angry. "That's it," I thought. I felt certain that he would not pass me for a paperwork error. "Please don't fail me for that" I thought.

At the end of the grading we all sat on the floor waiting to find out who had passed their examinations. As always a person's name would be read out and Sensei would bark either "Pass Shodan!" or "Try again". My name was one of the first to be read out which was quickly followed by a very loud "Pass Shodan". "Yes!" I said, clenching my fist, I had done it. Over thirty people attempted that day but only thirteen passed. The feeling was amazing. It was worth all the broken bones and bruises I had received over the years. I was the first 'Dan grade' aside from Gibi at our club.

I rang the store to share my good news. Friday afternoons were always busy and the store was full of customers. The owner Mr. Ford, got on the tannoy to announce, "Moray has got his Black Belt!" When I got home the next morning I went straight to a shop to purchase some black dye. I had worked hard for it and couldn't wait to put the Black Belt on. My picture was in the local paper and I was a bit of a celebrity for a while. People in the area knew I was a Black Belt and I basked in the glow of my success. I thought I had arrived. I now had to make sure to hold the grade and set the standards to the students at my club as an example for them to follow. I genuinely felt I had achieved something that was of real significance in my life for the first time ever. My confidence grew even more.

On returning home I asked my wife how her week had been and she mentioned that a new lad had joined the bank where she worked. She said she got on well with him. This was repeated in different ways over the next few weeks. Totally preoccupied with Karate and my job I didn't pay much attention to her comments.

A few weeks later I was called into Mr Ford's office and Mr Holland was there also. They explained that the branch manager of a national wholesale Cash and Carry was advertising for a buyer and an assistant manager. They recommended I should apply for a position, as I could go no further with them and they felt that it would be wrong to hold me back. I applied for the assistant manager's position and after a couple of tough interviews was offered the job. At the age of twenty I was the youngest assistant manager in a group of one hundred and twenty branches. The pay was £65 a week, which was a great deal of money at the time. My confidence and self esteem rose yet again. I was starting to become a legend in my own mind.

I left with the best wishes of Mr Ford and Mr. Holland and a gift from the staff. My first week was spent training at the seaside town of Paignton, South Devon. There at the local depot I learned the basic systems and company policies, before starting at the Barnstaple warehouse.

When I came back my wife was very different. Something had happened. She told me that she wanted to leave me and went to stay with her parents. She had been having an affair with her new work colleague. I genuinely wanted to kill him because my pride was hurt. She came back after a few days and saying she wanted to stay, so I took her back. It was then that I promised myself I would never let her hurt me again. In future I would look after 'number one' and if the opportunity for me to be unfaithful ever came, I would certainly take it.

When I started work at the Cash and Carry, nearly everyone knew me and called me by my first name, but the branch manager said that the staff would have to call me 'Mr McGuffie', which they did, but resentfully. It was difficult to start with. The manager Mr Thomas was a large overweight man. We got along well for the first couple of weeks. One afternoon, however, he came downstairs from his office and completely lost his temper. He threatened to sack me, because the staff hadn't got a delivery away quickly enough. I was totally shocked and couldn't believe my ears. I had been told off a few times before, but never in this way. I discovered that his management style was basically one of fear. He ruled the depot by controlling people. No one felt safe in his or her job and that included me as his deputy. He had what could be described as a split personality.

Every morning I could tell what sort of a day it was going to be by the way he arrived for work. If he went straight upstairs I knew it was going to be a bad day, if he came to see me and said "Hello" things would be okay. I never knew where I stood from one day the next. The next eighteen months were turbulent working with him. I kept my head down and did my best to ensure that I didn't have to face any more of his outbursts.

Chapter 6

Tooooooooooooooooot!

Unfortunately, during the time I worked with Mr Thomas, some of his aggressive attitude rubbed off onto me and as a result, I would make use his form of fear management to get the job done. I often harassed the staff to ensure that the checkouts were run properly and pushed all the staff in the different departments. This only made the staff resent me even more.

In the Cash and Carry we were all extremely surprised one day to learn that Mr. Thomas had been instantly dismissed for financial fraud. The position of branch manager was advertised throughout the company, which I immediately applied for. I didn't get the job because I was considered to be "too young" to run a branch at the age of twenty-two. This setback made me even more determined to achieve and prove my employers wrong. I was becoming extremely ambitious and wanted to be a senior manager.

A new branch manager, Martin Coles, was appointed. He was a great guy and I got on very well with him. He was there for about a year or so and eventually moved to join my old employer. He used to tell me stories of when he was a Special Patrol Group Police Officer in London. Some of the tales he told were incredible. We had fun together and he was a good boss. While he was there we did a massive refit of the store, which took three months. I worked between sixty and seventy hours every week in that period. When the job was finished he gave me extra paid time off, which I appreciated. When he left the position was advertised. I re-applied for the post but was again told that I was still too young, which frustrated me considerably.

I didn't have a full licence to drive a car on my own at the time, as I had not yet passed my driving test. I used to get a lift to work with our Butchery Manager, Terry Ford. He used to pick me up with his wife and children. They were a Christian family and his wife was one of those 'happy clappy people'. She would say things that irritated me, like "Praise the Lord" and "Thank you Jesus". She reminded me of the weird Christians I had seen on television some years before. I considered her and all other Christians to be the same type of people. I disliked them at all and believed that they were all weaklings that used Jesus as some sort of crutch. To me being a church goer was the total opposite of karate which had taught me about building self belief and inner strength, which was nothing like what I thought being a Christian was.

One Friday afternoon when we on our way home from work with Terry and his family, we got stuck in a traffic jam in the centre of the town. We were moving along very slowly in the car in a busy area. We came to a standstill behind a white Triumph Herald. A sign that was stuck on the lower middle part of the back window gradually came into focus. It read in bold print, **"TOOT IF YOU LOVE JESUS!"** "Oh no!" I thought, "Oh Please don't let her notice it there." She saw it and with a big smile on her face she said at the top of her voice, "Oh look, Praise the Lord!" I hoped that she would only give the horn a quick thump, but oh no, she waved to the person in the car in front and hit the horn long and hard "TOOOOOOOOOOOOOOOOOT!" I felt extremely embarrassed and believed everyone was staring at me. I wanted the ground to open up and swallow me. Everyone was laughing in the car except me. I sat there with my arms folded and had a look of total disgust on my face. I resented her for doing it and I even started walking to work because of it. On the odd occasion I saw her, it was very difficult for me to even speak to her.

My language was bad, I swore and cursed an awful lot. Like many people do today, I would use the name of Jesus as a swear word a great deal. I was speaking to Terry about business in his department one day and said "Jesus Christ" a few times during our conversation. Terry looked quite upset with me and pleaded with me, "Moray, please don't take the name of the Lord in vain". No one had ever said anything like that to me before. I thought it was funny, which made me do it even more. He almost begged me to stop but I wasn't having any of it. I knew his home was up for sale at the time, as he wanted to move house, so I said, "Do you want me to stop because Jesus is going to buy your house from you?" I could see that my words hurt him but I just didn't care and was pleased to have wound him up, in fact.

I was aged 22 when my wife became pregnant with our first daughter, Hannah. When she was born I was really delighted, a proud father and ran the two and a half miles home from the hospital in a suit and a heavy overcoat, overjoyed to have a little girl. In recent times I had been in more contact with my father by phone so I decided to ring him and tell him the news. When he answered I said, "Dad, we have just had a little girl and we have named her Hannah!" Very unenthusiastically he replied "Oh that's good." I was really excited and hoped that he would respond to it. His emotional detachment deeply wounded me.

Our conversations stopped from then on. It was to be the last time we spoke until I saw him on his death bed some years later. But he was too ill to even recognise me then. I very much regret my decision now. It would have been better to have been friends, at least, when he died; but the clock can't be turned back.

The responsibility of having a child plus the loss of my wife's income forced me to find extra work to cover the financial shortfall. I took extra jobs selling newspapers and even knocking doors to sell lottery tickets for a local football team. I did quite well and honed some of my selling skills. I developed a sales patter similar to that of a London market trader, which made people laugh and often resulted in a sale.

After Martin Coles left the Cash and Carry, a new manager named Ian Hambly was promoted to the position. He was just four years older than me and was very good at his job, even though he was extremely short sighted and colour blind. He had to use a magnifying glass, plus his glasses to read but he didn't let it affect his performance. We got on extremely well and he made me a promise that he would do all he could to help me to get a promotion. He was true to his word. We both worked very hard and built up the business considerably. I remember the first day that we took £100,000 – we both felt very pleased with ourselves and sat upstairs in the office after locking up, celebrating with a few cans of beer. He taught me a lot about management and how to 'trade the depot', as we called it. He helped to develop my management skills and that started to get me noticed with the people that mattered.

Our Regional Manager used to visit the depot occasionally. I always made sure that the store was looking immaculate when he came and that I spent some time with him. The trouble was that on every occasion he saw me he always got my name wrong! On meeting him I always had a bright smile on my face and said, while giving a firm handshake, "Hello, Mr Hutchings it's great to see you again". He was from the London area and his reply was always something like, "Ello, er, er, Arry" or, "Barry" or "Hi er, er, Marvin". It used to really irritate me but Ian would always cry with laughter when it happened. I did agree that it was funny and we spent many times laughing over it.

Despite Ian's best efforts to push me forward, Mr Hutchings failed to acknowledge my work. After a while though, new management came to our area. At last I was noticed at the age of twenty-four and was recommended to apply for two branch manager vacancies in Launceston in Cornwall and Weymouth in Dorset. The interview process was very challenging. Being young, plus the fact that I was up against very experienced managers from our region, realistically it seemed only a post at for the small site in Launceston might be a possibility. On completion of all of the interviews I was both surprised and delighted to discover that not only was I going to be promoted, but as manager of the newer and much larger Weymouth branch.

After I was given the news over the phone I went and told the staff who seemed very pleased for me. One group though, thinking that I was out of earshot, danced around and clapped their hands in the aisle in the knowledge that I was leaving. It wasn't very long before they wanted me back. The chap who replaced me was even more unpopular than I ever was!

A couple of weeks later, I pulled into the store car park in Weymouth on a bright sunny day with my Area Manager John Watts. He turned to me and said, "Well, there it is my boy". It was a large, new build, 20,000 square foot unit, which was about five minutes from the seaside. I had a tour and was introduced to all the staff. I then had a meeting with my Assistant Manager about the team, the area and the local competition, which I had already extensively researched. He was a pleasant chap in his fifties. The trouble was he didn't have any control of the personnel, or of the store, which was a mess. On top of that he was suffering with angina.

I was fired up, raring to go, extremely ambitious and wanting to make a name for myself. From my research I had already formulated a plan with the information I had obtained. I was motivated and excited I couldn't wait to get into the thick of it and I hoped that my enthusiasm was contagious. I asked John for his thoughts on how we could build the business and attack the competition. I will never forget his reply. "Oh, there isn't anything we can do to get more business as the competition has been here for years, we won't be able to touch them". I stood there in complete disbelief. The store was totally disorganised and lacking in effective management. If John had wanted to make an impression he certainly had, but unfortunately it was the wrong one. I decided that I would press ahead, with or without his support.

The place looked outdated and messy so I set about tidying it up. Everyone was pushed hard including my assistant manager who felt the strain and not long afterwards went on long term sick. That meant I now had to do both jobs and build up the business. I lived in a hotel for six weeks and went home at weekends. My house was sold quickly and my family moved to Weymouth. We lived on a caravan site for the summer then moved to a rented place before we bought our own house.

News had got out in the company that the Weymouth Branch Manager was a Black Belt at Karate. In fact it was on the front page of the company newsletter. The article said that any thieving customers had better watch out in case I had to use Karate on them. We had a young member of staff called Christopher Peach, who decided to have a go at me in an attempt to impress the other members of staff. One evening he waited for the store to close and hid himself away. I locked up the safe while a deputy manager waited for me at the front entrance. I turned off the lights, and it was pitch black. As I did that I sensed that there was someone still in the building. I had heard stories of criminals hiding in the dark and waiting for stores to close so that they could commit robbery and then break out. I felt certain that someone was there. I went ice cold and felt the hairs on the back on my neck stand up.

I stood motionless until my eyes started to get used to the blackness. I had learned this from reading Martial Arts books. Japanese Ninja warriors used to deliberately get chased in dark caves by enemies. Then they waited for their eyes to grow accustomed to the darkness. As the enemy ran in, they could strike and kill them. In similar manner I waited quietly for a few moments while my eyes re-adjusted. I then moved along very carefully in a fighting position, hands held at the ready, expecting someone to come at me from my right side. However, Christopher lunged at me from the left with a loud roar.

I reacted instantly, catching him powerfully on the side of his head with a 'spinning back roundhouse kick'. As it happened, my deputy manager, who was totally unaware of what was going on, opened the entrance door, which let a beam of light flood in. I will never forget that Chris was on the floor rubbing the side of his head with a painful expression on his face. He was fortunate that I had crepe soles on my shoes, otherwise I could have inflicted a serious injury. Word got around quickly amongst the staff and I never had any trouble with anyone after that.

When my wife and daughter had settled in Weymouth, I spoke to my instructor Gibi telling him that I had decided to open a Karate Club of my own, which I would run a couple of evenings a week. There was already a well-established club in the centre of the town run by a 2nd Dan (Second Degree Black Belt). His club was affiliated to the same association that I had received all of my grades from. I wanted to go on my own so I decided to join another group called 'Shotokan Karate International' headed in the UK by the famous Japanese Instructor Shiro Asano 7th Dan (Seventh Degree Black Belt). I had never trained with him but had read about him and knew that he was a very skilled instructor, with a phenomenal fighting record in Japan.

I set up training in a hall connected to a local pub called the Railway Inn, but it was only fifty yards from the existing

Karate club! I made sure that we didn't clash with the other club's training times. I organised sessions on Tuesday and Friday evenings as well as Sunday mornings. The numbers attending began to increase and I started a children's class. I placed an advertisement in the local paper. The father of one of the children who attended was a sign writer. He painted a huge sign with 'Weymouth Karate Do Shotokan' emblazoned across it. Shotokan is a style of Karate. The pub owner gave me permission to fit it to the outside wall.

Posters of me performing a flying kick were placed all over the town to advertise the club. Things were going well with new students joining each week. I had a number of phone calls about Karate sessions and so on. One evening, a man rang after seeing an advert in the newspaper. I explained about the club and what the charges were, training times. I always asked questions about the person's age, physical fitness and the reason for learning Karate. I got answers like "I want to get fit", or "to build up my confidence". When I was as satisfied as I could be with the answers I always asked a final question which was to discover whether the person had ever been in trouble with the police for any act of violence. When I asked one man, the answer he gave was unbelievable and shocked me to the core. He replied "Well I got into a fight and the police tried to break it up, so I beat up a few policemen". "How many did you actually beat up?" He replied "Seven". I said to him "Well why do you need to learn Karate?" I didn't invite him along to train.

During one evening session, a large, stocky man with long blond hair and a very mean look on his face walked through the door, sat down and watched the session. It was obvious that he was finding fault. When the training had finished I decided to go over to him and introduce myself. I did not recognise him but he told me that he was the instructor from the club up the road. He was extremely aggressive and wanted to know how I had the audacity to open a club nearby in his town! He was red in the face and very angry. We stood toe-to-toe and nose-to-nose shouting at each other. He wanted me to move my club. I told him that there was no way that I would. All of my students stood and watched in silence. I was ready for a fight and my fists were clenched. There was no way that I was going to back down, especially with everyone watching. Eventually he just swore and left. I never saw him again.

I got my first twelve students ready to take their first grading exam. I wrote to Sensei Asano and arranged a date for him to visit the club. I pushed everyone very hard over the next few weeks and made sure that I had instilled good Dojo Kun (Rules of the training hall) into the students. They all showed good Karate etiquette and had a strong fighting spirit. The day soon arrived. I waited outside the hall well before the pre-arranged time to meet him. The students were all waiting patiently in the hall and were lined up like soldiers. Eventually he pulled up in a green VW camper van with his wife and three children. They went to the beach for the afternoon while we went into the changing room. Sensei Asano asked in his very broken English, "How many student grading?" I replied "Just twelve Sensei, all White Belts and me". He gave a huge bellowing laugh and answered "White Belto very good, no answer back. Ha ha ha!" I agreed, nodding and bowing all of the time that he was speaking.

During the session I put in all the effort and energy that I could. When I stood still for just a few seconds, the sweat dripped off the end of my nose and formed small puddles on the floor! All the time Sensei Asano would be shouting "More Quick!" and "Strongo!" Everyone there tried their hardest. Eventually, Sensei Asano finished that part of the session and shouted, "Kohon Abi!" which meant we could rest. We all sat cross-legged in a straight line close to the wall. I had just sat down when Sensei looked at me and yelled "Black Belt!" "Oss Sensei!" I replied. I quickly stood up, bowed, sprinted out, bowed again and stood waiting for my next instruction. Sensei then stood in a free fighting position and said, "Free style, we fight now". I knew that meant we were going to be doing this at full speed and power. As I readied myself a flash back came to me of reading an article of how he fought all of his Black Belt students, and gave each one a beating. I thought to myself "Oh no, I'm in for it now". Smack! I was flat on the floor. He had delivered a roundhouse kick to the head at full speed; I didn't see it I just felt a throbbing pain down the side of my face. I looked at him as he walked away. The next twenty minutes consisted of me getting one of the biggest thrashings of my life. He literally wiped the floor with me. I managed to hit him twice. He just dodged and moved out of the way of every technique I threw at him. He caught me so many times that I lost count. My students sat with their mouths wide open. One student said that it was like watching a movie.

The lesson finished and those who wanted to take a grading examination waited in the hall while we changed. I looked at myself in the mirror. My face was as red as a beetroot. My body was covered with a mass of red marks where I had been hit time after time. I plucked up the courage and asked "Sensei, could I please have your permission to attempt Nidan (2nd degree Black Belt) at this year's summer course?". His reply was "Yesu, you havu very gudr style". "Thank you very much Sensei" was my answer as I bowed deeply. I felt like a million dollars. Especially as I found out later on that he very rarely complimented any of his students, even the ones that won European and World titles in competition.

The grading went very well and we had a 100% pass rate. I thanked him for his time and looked forward to seeing him again. He had a major impact on my life over the next few years. I held him in great respect and took every opportunity I could to train with him, travelling all over the country to do so. My ability, technique and understanding of Karate grew dramatically over the next few years under his guidance and instruction.

The changes I made in the store had a rapid and positive effect on sales and we gained new customers. When I took over the branch my brief was to maintain the losses it had made and not to increase them. There was about six months of the financial year remaining when I took over. During that time the loss was wiped out and a healthy profit made. As a result I became a bit of a superstar in the company. This did wonders for my self-esteem and brought the praise and recognition that I had sought since childhood. The store targets for the next year were substantially increased but I exceeded them again! In eighteen months I had increased turnover by 150% and was now making substantial profits for the group. My branch was being lined up for conversion to a new type of Cash and Carry.

A big meeting was arranged for the Regional Director to visit my store to discuss a possible conversion to a new mega-depot. A few days before this, my area manager visited me and gave me a long list of jobs to do to get the warehouse tidier for the big visit. One of the jobs was to paint the outside customer toilet doors red. On the big day, it was the last remaining job. I instructed a young man to paint them and put up a 'Wet Paint' sign. He did the painting, locked the doors but forgot to put the sign up. My bosses arrived earlier than arranged after a three-hour drive. My area manager desperately needed to use the toilet and ran from the car to the public toilets! He pushed at the locked door. Moments later he came into the warehouse in a rage. The palms of his hands were covered in bright red paint and so was the end of his nose! The Regional Manager had to stay in his car for an hour because he couldn't stop laughing. The amusing story got around quickly and my boss never really forgave me. From that day his attitude towards me changed.

The sales and profits I achieved were very good indeed, but the pressure was massive. As a manager you had to be constantly looking over your shoulder – sackings and demotions seemed to happen all of the time, pressure to perform was intense. I began to feel that I no longer wanted to go to work. The truth was that I hated it. The figures were still very good, but we were now just too busy, and were being stretched to the limit.

The company sent a more mature and experienced man to be my assistant manager. Jimmy Thomson was from Scotland, was a terrific guy with a great deal of experience. He was over sixty when he joined and we worked well together. The only problem was that he had a very quick temper and used to fly off the handle with staff and customers. We still continued to do well as a branch but I didn't enjoy it any more and obviously disliked the amount of pressure branch managers were under. To escape from the pressure I started to consider other job opportunities.

Chapter 7

Another direction

I went to Nottingham University for a summer training camp that was held by Sensei Asano. I trained very hard throughout the week, aware that Sensei was watching me closely. The day of the grading arrived and there were only a few people attempting 2nd Dan. The examinations on basics and combinations went well. With hopeful anticipation we waited for the results to be declared. My name was read out and Sensei shouted, "Pass Nidan" (2nd Dan). I was elated; it was a significant achievement. I couldn't wait to get home to my club to tell my students. It was another box ticked in my mind. Without realising it I had become very goal orientated. Having a plan with an aim in every area of my life made sense to me; a focused determination began that day when Mr Morgan advised me to give up playing the trombone and grew when working under Brian Ford. Over the years this certainly became fixed in my mind: hard work produced results and in turn promotion, a higher salary and all the trappings of success.

My self confidence soared. I gradually became obsessed with my achievements, I took great pleasure in the recognition and respect others now showed towards me because of my success. The news of me attaining 2nd Dan was reported in the local press once again and my fame spread. More success at Karate meant more income and security. My Karate club was now very successful with ninety adults and fifty children regularly training there. I sold Karate uniforms, belts and other equipment that I sourced wholesale. It made sense to consider teaching on a professional basis, and opening a shop retailing Martial Arts equipment. The search began in earnest for suitable premises and to expand my teaching by holding additional classes. Then came the discovery of a new shopping centre about to open in Weymouth. I started making plans to have a martial arts shop there.

I read somewhere that the only way to earn serious money was to become self-employed. Wealthy customers came into the Cash and Carry; they were successful working in their own businesses, whilst I had built a strong business for my employers. Why couldn't I do it myself? Discussing my intentions with some friends, they expressed many reservations, especially that of leaving the security of well paid employment. Despite their lack of belief in me, I stated firmly that my mind was set on my goal. I was determined to "Go for it and be a success in my own business". Utterly focused on my objective and I sincerely believed that applying the same principles that I used in my job and Karate would guarantee success in my own business. It did, for a while. However I hadn't done enough ground work expecting my business to thrive on effort. It was a big risk to take because of poor planning on my part. The experience taught me some hard lessons about the business world that I would need to remember.

The phrases I came across in later years proved true in my case at this time and would again in the future. The first being: *Prior preparation and planning prevent a poor performance.* Secondly: *People don't plan to fail, they just fail to plan.*

The time came for me to resign from my job at the Cash and Carry I was absolutely delighted and ready for a new challenge. In the same week it was announced that I had won a National Sales Competition based on business generated per square foot of a new own label range. The prize was a family holiday for two weeks in Barbados, which sadly I had to decline! I sent my resignation letter in by post and didn't hear from my area manager for about a week. When he finally contacted me, he evidently was not impressed. His resentment was obvious and he insisted I work the full notice period, which was extremely unusual. Normally any branch manager that resigned would be asked to leave the same day. At the final Regional Managers' meeting which I was ordered to attend, my boss John Watts pointedly announced with heavy sarcasm that I was leaving the company because I thought I could earn more money teaching Karate. Furious at his comments I vowed to myself, "Right mate, I will show you".

I informed my students of my intention to become a professional instructor. I was pleased with their enthusiastic response. I established a second new group in Blandford Forum, Dorset, which proved to be successful too. The standard there proved to be higher over time because there were fewer students so they benefited from more individual tuition. In the classes I ran there, I met a girl there who was always friendly and chatty. Attracted by the warmth of her personality, we became friends and then later began an affair. I reasoned that it was okay because I had been hurt in the past in the same way. Keeping that promise to myself from some years earlier, I took advantage of the opportunity when it came along. For a few months my head was in the clouds. We exchanged love letters and the folly of keeping mine got me into trouble later on.

I raised money to open my retail business called 'Kihaku Martial Arts Supplies' in the new indoor shopping centre in Weymouth. The word Kihaku means "Fighting Spirit". The shop got steady trade and did reasonably well, but I realised after a few months that it was never going to make me a fortune. I enjoyed running the shop though. It had an extensive book section and I read most of them during the quiet periods, gaining a greater understanding of different fighting styles and systems. This knowledge became very useful when advising customers on their purchases. Besides selling books, I sold martial arts uniforms, martial arts weapons, replica guns and training equipment. I also specialised in the sale of replica Samurai swords as the ways of the Samurai Warrior interested me greatly. Something I hadn't envisaged was that the shop would be a magnet for some very strange people.

Once I was asked outside to fight with a guy who came into the shop wearing a kimono with a samurai sword in his belt. Over time I became accustomed to people coming in and acting aggressively. A couple of my customers said that they were very highly graded Martial Artists, which was not the truth but they kept up the deception. I had one particularly scary event. I was on the telephone speaking to a customer with my back to the sales area. When I turned around a samurai sword was pointing close to my face. A dirty-looking man with long hair and a beard stood there holding the sword with outstretched arms. I had never seen him before. He had removed the sword from a display and was shouting at me aggressively, "I know who you are". He kept repeating it and then said, "Look, I can have you any time I want". It was tense to say the least, but thankfully after a few minutes he put the sword down. It ended with us laughing and joking together. He eventually left the shop and I never saw him again.

One morning a young man came in and bought a replica Heckler and Kotch machine gun that was made of plastic and fired soft plastic pellets. He paid cash for it and left the shop. About an hour later, two policemen came in to ask if I had recently sold the gun. I informed them that I had. Then they described the incident that had occurred after the young man left my shop. He had gone straight to the Post Office and carried out an attempted armed robbery! The cashier realised that the gun wasn't real, and pressed the silent alarm that went off at the Police Station. Officers quickly turned up and arrested him.

To promote the shop and clubs further I arranged a couple of Martial Arts Extravaganzas and filled a couple of theatres with avid Martial Arts fans. The finales were always by my club. We performed a number of demonstrations culminating in a pre-arranged group fight sequence, all of which was performed to Japanese music. We received favourable newspaper reports as a result.

While running the Karate clubs and the shop I was ill on a couple of occasions. The first time I had a chest virus, which drained me of all my energy. I was not able to teach for a month and the number of students in the classes reduced significantly. I still had a weakness from childhood asthma, which has continued to this day. The second time I caught measles. Very ill and unable to work or teach for several weeks meant that sales slumped in the business and the numbers in the classes dropped substantially. It took me a while to regain my fitness. I had to cut back somewhere, so during the late summer of 1985 I gave the Blandford club to one of my students and closed the shop.

I hadn't failed at anything for quite some time and so I was surprised by this turn of events. Up until then I had considered myself invincible, always thinking that I could do anything if I put my mind to it. The fact was that I had failed, it was as simple as that, but it was hard to accept failure.

I started looking for something else to do work wise, as I needed income quickly. In the Situations Vacant section of the local paper was an advert, which read:

"FINANCIAL ADVISERS REQUIRED. NO EXPERIENCE NEEDED AS FULL TRAINING WILL BE PROVIDED. INCOME £8,000 - £12,000 PER ANNUM".

We needed money urgently so I thought "What do I have to lose, why not give it a try?" The advert gave a choice of two names to contact and I rang the second one. His name was Mickey Rafferty and perhaps I called him rather than the first one because of my own Celtic roots. I assumed from his name that he might be young. We had a chat and a brief interview over the phone after which he invited me into his offices in Poole for a more formal meeting. We discovered that we were the same age, like minded and soon became firm friends. Little did I know that the meeting would lead to success and enormous lifestyle changes for me over the next seven years.

I was about to start an incredible period of exponential growth that even I could never have imagined. I was heading for the top!

My mother and father in Dublin around 1950

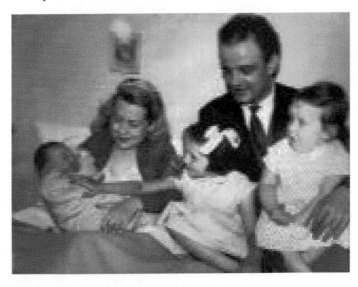

The newspaper picture on the day of my birth with my mother
And father and my sisters Kathryn and Lorraine

My father as I will always remember him

Writing music with my father

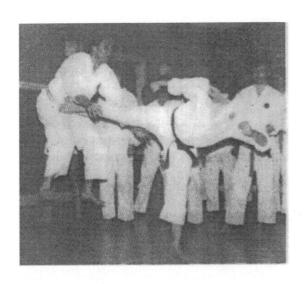

Me demonstrating a side kick for a karate magazine on one of
my students. The caption said "Don't be late again"

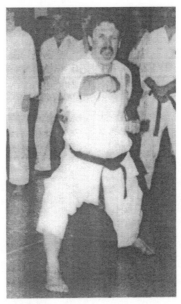

Another magazine photo

Beware of the manager!

ANY light-fingered customers at Gardners (Bristol) cash & carry Weymouth depot had better beware.

New manager, Moray McGuffie has a black belt in karate.

"I was inspired when I saw Bruce Lee's tactics in the film *Enter The Dragon*," said Moray.

That was 10 years ago, when he was 15 years old, and since then he has progressed through the various standards — different coloured belts awarded for skill and technique.

The secret of karate does not lie in the famous chop according to Moray. It's the accuracy and skill in performing the kick and the punch.

"Karate began more than 1,000 years ago on the island of Okinawa in Japan. No weapons were allowed on the island and the people used karate to protect themselves and disarm enemies," he explained.

Karate became a fashionable sport in the 1940's with various styles emerging. He is an enthusiast of the traditional Sho To Kan method which he describes as "the most dynamic and powerful form of karate".

Teaching

Moray learned the sport at a karate club in Branstaple and later turned to instruction, teaching classes of up to 60 students.

Since his move to Weymouth, Moray has not joined a karate club. "I'm looking around to assess the standard in the area before I decide which club to join," he added.

Chapter 8

Upward Spiral

I went through a series of three interviews with Mickey Rafferty who was from Ireland. An ex-Royal Marine who had fought in the Falklands war, Mickey had been recently promoted as manager of a team of four people for a company called FPS Management Ltd. At my final interview he kept lifting my job application form up to read and did not realise that his writing on the back of it was visible to me. There was a fairly large section at the bottom of it for manager's comments. He had written, *"OUTSTANDING!"* in large block capitals, so I knew that he was going to offer me a position.

The job was based in Poole, Dorset in a large office block very near to the well-known harbour, a thirty-minute journey from my home. The position involved selling financial services products on a commission only basis. We sold regular monthly premium savings plans, lump sum investments, pensions and life assurance. Many advisers also arranged mortgages, general insurance, loans and business finance too. Every client's situation was different which meant dealing with a large variety of products. This made the job very interesting. Keeping up with the investment markets and studying for exams as well as reading up on the latest developments took up a lot of my time.

A new adviser always started with a number of their own contacts (normally at least fifty), which led onto building a client bank through recommendation and prospecting. I enjoyed the initial fortnight of training, and then I was allowed to meet the public. I still managed to run the Karate club in Weymouth and over time the number of students rose again.

I started working as a Financial Adviser in October 1985. The first month involved only two weeks' selling; I came in second place for sales in the office, which surprised me. The next month, I came second in the whole region. Returning from working a weekend away in Barnstaple having sold 15 different contracts set a record for one day in the branch. The people in the team were amazed, so I was asked to give a short speech at the end-of-month regional meeting. I spoke for just a couple of minutes and was extremely nervous about it.

I found the job fitted my penchant for selling. I really enjoyed the buzz of the business and working alongside high achievers. My desire was not just as good as they were, but to be even better. I had developed a very competitive edge. I loved the praise and recognition that I received in this type of business environment. My first cheque for two weeks' work was £779, I was thrilled. My second pay cheque was due just before Christmas and did not arrive until the last evening before the festive break. With very little money in the bank, by the end of the day I started feeling down-hearted, imagining that the paycheque wouldn't arrive until after Christmas. We had bought nothing for the festivities so I was hoping for commission of £1,000. The envelope finally arrived and to my great surprise contained a cheque for £2,559, which was a lot of money in 1985. I was elated and drove home like a madman.

Shopping for the Christmas goodies it felt like I had struck gold, but I wanted to do even better. I continued to remind myself that I could go to the top if I put my mind to it. I had done it before, so I knew that I could do the same again.

The atmosphere in the office was always very positive and at times involved bullying the slacker people to get them generating sales. There were twenty advisers there plus three managers. Mickey's team grew steadily and very soon I was ready to qualify to go into management because of the business that I had generated and due to the fact that I had also personally recruited two new advisers into the branch as it was a requirement for a promotion.

A large amount of time was spent on training and practice. We studied sales techniques, closing a sale, dealing with objections and presentation skills. Appointment making ideas were drummed into us almost every day. We had appointment making sessions where all of the office chairs were piled up in the middle of the office. Advisers weren't allowed to get a chair to sit down on at their desk until they had arranged a minimum of five meetings. The atmosphere in these sessions was always competitive with bottles of wine being given away as prizes. There was generally a lot of shouting, cheering, teasing and mickey-taking.

One negative point about the industry and others like it was that there was a very high turnover of advisers who didn't make the grade. It was sad to see many people who had become friends have to leave, but we pressed forward, focused on earning more money and soon forgot about them. There was such tremendous comradeship in the team; it was above anything that I had experienced before. We always supported each other and enjoyed each other's company. Perhaps it was the fact the team consisted of ex-Marines and ex-Special Boat Squadron marines that created that atmosphere of camaraderie.

Every week the Regional Manager visited the office and on one such visit I had a meeting with him. His name was Nigel Prior and he was earning around £7,000 a month at the time. That seemed like a Film Star's wages to me and he drove a Porsche! He asked what I wanted to do with my career. As confident as ever I told him that I wanted his job. To my astonishment he said that I could have it and he even asked me when I wanted it! "As quickly as possible," I replied. He told me it would take at least seven years. Unable to resist the challenge I vowed to beat that period, telling Him I would beat the time he had set me.

Our team moved to Weymouth to open a new branch office and within a couple of months I had a sales team of ten advisers and had qualified as a branch manager progressing through four promotions in a record time. I was now involved in the sales training of all new recruits, which I thoroughly enjoyed. All of my sessions used humour and were well received. One afternoon I was called to Mickey's office, as he wanted to speak to me about the training. I wondered if there was some problem with my teaching style. He told me that he had received very good feedback from the trainees and that they enjoyed my sessions most of all. My delight knew no bounds and my self esteem grew further.

I was still training and teaching at my Karate club in Weymouth. I decided to leave Sensei Asano's organisation to join another one which charged lower fees. The move also meant that I would be able to conduct my own grading examinations up to 1st Dan Black Belt. I went to Liverpool to attempt 3rd Dan together with a student of mine who was attempting 1st Dan. It meant a very early start to reach our destination by 10am. We had a long wait for the examiner, a 6th Dan, as he hadn't been informed of our arrival. That afternoon we went though a very demanding examination. We performed a large amount of basics with long combinations of techniques, then many different types of sparring and ending with competition style freestyle fighting. During this section a whole Aikido class stopped their training at the other end of the hall to watch us fight.

The examiner passed us both, commending us for our high standard of technique. However, he also told me off because I hadn't shaved that morning and said that I looked scruffy. Being a 3rd Dan meant being at another level, that of a Master. I was delighted once again with this achievement, which made me the highest graded Karate instructor in our area.

At work business was still going very well and I was allowed to open my own branch in Yeovil in Somerset. My income had increased to around £4,000 a month. I decided to reward myself and changed my car, which was a dented white Ford Capri to a brand new willow green metallic Mercedes saloon which was a pleasure to drive. My neighbours were very surprised and some were envious of I loved the feeling of driving expensive cars, especially those that were known as Marques. As soon as I bought the first, I began planning to buy a bigger and more expensive one.

Another thing I enjoyed was buying expensive business suits, overcoats, shirts, ties, silk handkerchiefs and shoes. Maybe the reason stemmed back to having to wear those awful knitted jumpers at school!

My branch grew and soon there were ninety advisers. It became the number one office in the company and won me the title of Branch Manager of the Year. I opened two further branches in Taunton and Cardiff and was promoted to Regional Manager and then General Manager equalling Nigel' position. He remained in charge of the overall region and was earning a lot more than me. What he said would take seven years I accomplished in two, now earning around £10,000 a month. I was quick to let him know what I had achieved. He was genuinely delighted because all my promotions had helped to push his income way above mine.

We moved from our three bedroom terraced house to a large detached executive house in a lovely village in the countryside near Yeovil. Our beautiful new home was made from hand cut sandstone and set in a very select cul-de-sac. It was a very exciting time, delightedly we furnished the house just the way we wanted it. I bought two more new cars, a much bigger black metallic sporty Mercedes for me and a black metallic BMW for my wife. I revelled in being successful and able to buy whatever I wanted. Shopping and spending money soon became favourite habits that were extremely hard to end.

News spread around the company about me, resulting in me travelling to other regions as a keynote speaker giving motivational speeches. My talks consisted of a lot of hype, PMA (Positive Mental Attitude) and plenty of jokes. People always laughed when I spoke. I was now reaping the benefit of being a joker in my youth, able to talk about even difficult or complicated subjects by injecting humour into them. As my reputation grew, the number of speaking engagements also increased.

The whole of the company's business was built on the positive mental attitude approach. Mantra-like phrases were ingrained in us such as: -

"By the inch it's a cinch, by the yards it's hard"
"You can if you think you can"
"Success comes in cans, not in cannots"
"If you think you can't you are right, because you won't"
"Have a Positive Mental Attitude"
"What your mind can conceive and believe it will achieve"
"Quitters never win and winners never quit"

Those phrases became incantations that we would say over and over again to our team members.

The National Sales Manager Ron Donaldson coined the one that affected me most of all. He was a multi-millionaire earning an astonishing, £140,000 a month at his peak. His mantra was, "Think, act, believe and become".

He said to me one day "Moray, if you think like a millionaire, then act like a millionaire. Believe that you will become a millionaire and you will become a millionaire". That is exactly what I wanted to hear. I aspired to be like him so I did exactly what he said, continually saying to myself, "Think act, believe and become". I especially practiced this before an important meeting.

Ron had a great influence on me. He always said that we were different from others. His advice to me was to remind myself every day that I wasn't like other people, to walk down the stairs backwards in the morning and tie my shoelaces the opposite way. I followed his methods in every way. When confronted with a business problem, we would even say in all seriousness, "What would Ron do"?

I got so involved in my job that I started attending my Karate classes less and less and eventually gave the club away to a couple of my senior students. My focus was on myself, my career and how much money I could earn. I was in a meeting with my boss one day and got so excited about my potential income that I wrestled him to the floor.

We used to laugh and say things like, "I wonder what the poor people are doing today?" Our obsession with money seems like madness when I think back. I remember Mickey said once "I am earning more than I could ever have imagined, but I just want even more". We laughed hysterically about it. I felt exactly the same way he did. I wanted more myself! My income gave me a power that I had never experienced before.

I am grateful to never have had alcohol or drug habits but realise upon reflection that I was a type of addict. I had an addiction to power, success and what money could do for me. They were like a fix I needed desperately and resulted in me being on a high most of the time. I was totally driven, constantly living my life at a very high pace, entirely focused on how I could earn more, buy more expensive items and build wealth.

To build my region I held recruitment seminars in cities and towns late into the evenings at least three a times week. I often had a long drive home, getting back very late. I then had to leave the house at 6am the next morning and so I rarely saw my children. Constant working, speaking and driving started to wear me out. I decided to stay in Wales a couple of days a week and started living out of a suitcase. It was acceptable at first, but then the novelty wore off. I changed my Mercedes for a blue Porsche 928 S2 that I loved to pose in. It was an impressive, fast, noisy car, exactly the same model and colour that my boss Nigel had. When he saw me driving it, he changed his for a red Ferrari.

After a while my immediate manager Mickey became unpopular with his senior managers due to his management style, which was to control by fear. He was pulled aside on a number of occasions by the senior management team and told to sort himself out, which he did for a while. However, eventually he was forced to resign. I was to report to Nigel Prior who was earning an incredible £30,000 a month by then.

I attended a convention in Toronto with the top achievers in the company. One morning I was summoned to the chairman's suite, whose name was Michael Ravens. He remains to this day the most frightening man I have ever worked with. He was an outstanding achiever and had a strong vision for the company that he had built. Nigel Prior and Ron Donaldson were also in the room with him.

For the first fifteen minutes or so of our meeting Ron and Nigel attacked me verbally about my overconfidence saying my rise up the promotional ladder was too quick for my own good. They wore me down with all of their criticisms. Eventually, much to my relief, Michael interrupted and said that they should stop. Then in a caring tone said, "Moray, do you remember when I flew down in a helicopter to speak at one of your regional meetings?". "Yes I do Michael"; I replied thinking "Great, at least he must believe in me". He continued "You gave a speech that day on goal planning didn't you?" Would you like to know what I thought of what you said?" "Yes please" I said enthusiastically. Michael then went as red as a beetroot and the veins stood out on the side of his neck as he shouted "I thought it was the biggest!!***!!!** !! that I have ever heard!" I sat there utterly confused wondering what on earth was going on.

There was a pause…

Then grinning broadly Nigel said "Moray, all of that aside we have decided to promote you and put you in charge of Wales as well as your own region, congratulations!" I sat there with my mouth wide open in surprise. What they had just done was to hammer down the nail somewhat, as Sensei Asano did when I passed my 2nd Dan - he visited my club and picked me up on everything I did that was not quite perfect in front of my students to let me know that there was more to achieve. I sat in the room with my bosses and we all laughed and joked about what they had just put me through. I left the room that morning floating on air. The promotion would bring even greater income.

This was it; I had very quickly become one of the most senior and respected managers in the business. From that day on nicknamed "Quantum Leap" by Nigel, I believed that I really was a superstar. The trouble was that it was entirely in my own mind. I had beaten all of the goals and targets that I had set myself and felt is if I was unstoppable.

We were taught as managers and advisers to plan and write goal lists. We had to think about the items we really wanted like cars, houses, holidays and so on. Then they suggested we stick pictures of the items all around the house, especially in the bathroom and in our Filofax to constantly remind us of what we were trying to achieve.

In the early days I had a picture of a plane and Disney World in Florida on the door of a kitchen cupboard and bathroom mirror. I would see it many times every day as a reminder of what I wanted to do. I set up a plan made of targets to achieve each month which meant I could save money towards the holiday. Every time I hit a target it acted as a boost to reach the next one. In fact, my aim for a twelve month period I achieved in just seven months! This further cemented my belief in setting goals.

When we went on holiday there, the feeling of achievement was absolutely amazing. I remember driving my hire car and turning on the radio. The announcer said "Hi this is Rock and Roll Radio USA". I thought to myself "Yes! I have done it!" and was feeling on top of the world. *Little did I know that on this holiday, I would have my first genuine encounter with the Gospel of Jesus Christ.*

Chapter 9

A living legend in my own mind

In the very early hours of my first Sunday morning on holiday in the USA, I woke up and turned on the television while my wife and my daughters Hannah and Megan were still asleep. I sat up in bed and flicked through the channels for something interesting to watch. I stopped on a programme, which appeared to have on it a motivational speaker, watching with interest until I realised that it was based at a church and the speaker was a Television Evangelist. "Oh no, not one of those Christians again!" I said to myself. But there was something different about this man and his manner that grabbed my attention. This American spoke about Jesus, quoting scriptures. His confidence and obvious belief in what he was speaking about left a profound impression on me. Having spoken at events and business meetings myself, I liked the way he moved around the platform. He raised his voice sometimes as he delivered his message and at one point he picked up his Bible and waved it at the congregation. He talked about what he called 'The Truth' and compared it with other belief systems. He had great interaction with his audience, which I liked.

He pointed to a scripture and then prodded the Bible very hard as he said "If you want to know the truth about life, I am saying if it ain't in the Bible then don't believe it." He then moved around the stage holding up his Bible in silence for a few moments. I had never seen or heard anything like it before and thought it was very different from the type of boring preaching I had heard when I attended in church as a child, or for weddings and funerals. Sitting through those meetings had been like watching paint dry. *Observing this man though, something significant happened in my mind, because I found myself saying "I need to buy myself one of those Bibles tomorrow".*

For the first time in my life, perhaps because of the way the speaker delivered his message, I thought that there must be something to this Christian stuff. Maybe it wasn't as boring as I had thought it was. The few times I had been in church I disliked it immensely and found the vicar's sermon boring. I had thought how easy it was to fall asleep during the service. The speaker I had been watching was both funny and serious, but what had grasped my attention was his passion. He didn't speak in the same way as the vicars I had heard in the past, who droned on in slow, deep monotonous voices. It was obvious that this speaker totally believed in what he was talking about. It was actually very inspiring which shocked me. When the programme ended I looked through the other channels and was disappointed that I couldn't find anything else similar.

That day I made my way to a large bookshop, headed for the religious section and found what I was looking for. There was a large selection of Bibles, different sizes, print fonts, quality, and translations. I remembered that the preacher on television had a Bible that appeared to be a high quality, soft leather version. "I want one the same as that," I thought, looking for the most expensive there. I picked one up and examined the quality. As I was doing this, a man came and stood next to me, browsing through the section. I immediately felt under pressure thinking, "What on earth are you doing? Put it back!" Embarrassed and not wanting anyone to see me holding a Bible, I quickly put it back onto the shelf and made a sharp exit from the shop.

On returning to work after the holiday I found that my sales region had continued to grow. I was now attending the Top Ten Managers' meetings. Although earning a very high income, my sales figures were just under the level required to qualify for these high level meetings at our Head Office. However my manager, Nigel, allowed me to attend some of them, no doubt to motivate me further. I really enjoyed the meetings, mixing with high achievers, picking up ideas and putting forward my point of view. I would often look around the boardroom and set myself targets to beat the other regional managers. I wanted to be the best and more than that, for everyone to recognise it.

Nigel told me that I had to attain the required sales target for the following month in order to come to the next meeting. I didn't take what he had said seriously. The end of the month came and we had just missed the critical sales figure again. He rang me on a Friday evening at home and said "Moray, I am taking you off the meetings". Totally devastated I put down the phone. Furious with myself, I vowed "He will never do that to me again". The next month was one of unrelenting pressure for the managers below me. I set high targets for each office and drove them incredibly hard for the whole month. My region produced a 50% increase in sales, smashing all previous records by miles.

This result ensured my place at the meetings again. December was quiet, a short business month due to the Christmas holidays, but in January we increased sales by a further 50%, even further in February and yet another very significant increase in March. The day the March figures were released I was in a hotel setting up the hall for a regional meeting with one of my training staff. When my Personal Assistant came in and told me the new record we had achieved, I ran around cheering and waving my arms like I had just scored a winning goal at Wembley. I literally sprinted around the whole hall, which was massive. The call from Nigel had been a shrewd move because he knew that it was recognition and power that motivated me. He had certainly pressed the right button. Over a period of four months my region had increased its sales production by over 250%. More speech invitations from around the country followed and I believed that I was a megastar.

The results increased my self-esteem so much that I was becoming a legend in my own mind. It is hard to explain how I felt – just on top of the world and that failure was simply not even a possibility. I felt I could stop a train at full speed with just one word. Once again, planning followed by effort produced results. Renowned all over the country I was asked to appear on company videos and loved the limelight, the fame, the kudos, the money and most of all the great feeling of power it gave me.

To build the business further I decided to concentrate on training advisers and managers to be more effective. I devised a system of sales that was nicknamed the "Diamond Method." The name came about because one of my other nicknames was "Diamond Geezer", because I often wore flashy jewellery. The training programme worked spectacularly. I believed this proved I was the star of the company and I became increasingly self obsessed. It was all about **ME**. I wanted more success, more cash, more cars, and more houses, in fact more of everything.

The country's economy was peaking, and I was taking every advantage of it; but history has evidenced many times that 'Boom' is often followed by 'Bust'. The company didn't plan for a poor trading period and neither did I. In fact the thought never entered my mind because we were riding the crest of the wave called success. Considering that one of our most used phrases in the company was "People don't plan to fail, they just fail to plan", we were not listening to the advice that we gave to everyone else. More importantly, I should have learned from my past mistakes. Unfortunately, I just carried on believing that the success just would never stop.

At one senior managers' meeting Nigel jokingly suggested that the company change our job titles from regional manager and the like to something that reflected our positions. He said "How about Moray McGuffie Fairly Rich, Nigel Prior Quite Rich and Ron Donaldson Very Rich". We were "living on another planet" as the saying goes.

We were instructed to listen to motivational tapes while we were driving as we spent so much time behind the wheel. This made sense to me, so I bought some tapes by a very well known speaker called Zig Ziglar from Texas and some others by Jim Roan. Unbeknown to me both of these men were Christians. They both mentioned verses from the Bible in their messages. Jim was a bit more subtle, but Zig was totally unabashed, not caring if it grated on the listener. On one particular tape he recounted a person once asking him how he could get on in life. "If you want to get on in life young man, then you must first get right with God" was his reply. "What does that mean, getting right with God?" I asked myself. Whatever he meant, the truth was that I didn't like hearing it. I had forgotten all about the preacher on early morning TV in USA. When I heard these speakers talk about God and Jesus, I would remember Terry Ford and his wife and the dreaded car horn. The memory still made me cringe. My own pre-conceived ideas that all Christians were weaklings remained. "That stuff is definitely not for me" I would say.

My sales figures and my income still continued to climb as I was given yet more responsibility. The company grew as well but it was at much too rapid a pace. There was so much business going into the Head Office that the staff there could not process it all. Cases that had normally taken a week to result in payment of commission were taking two or three months. This meant payments slowed down and people started to leave the company. The knock on effect was that no one serviced the clients, which in turn led to cancellation of policies so that commission was reclaimed from us, totally wiping out pay cheques in many cases.

By this time I had five flashy cars – BMWs, Jaguars and Porsches on my drive, I had massive outgoings and a very high spending lifestyle, so I started to run up a large overdraft at the bank. I was even called into see the bank manager a couple of times. Looking back I can see that I was a complete hypocrite because I prayed to God on the way to the bank in the car asking, "God please help me and please let the manager extend my overdraft." Each time that it was extended I quickly forgot about God until the next time I had to see the bank manager. The country's economy started to decline and the daily news was of firms cutting back or even worse, going into liquidation and of the increasing level of unemployment.

My financial situation worsened dramatically. From having not been a worrier for a long time I started losing sleep because of all my problems. I didn't want to lose all that I had built up. I rang Nigel and said I needed to talk through a few problems. We met at a hotel and I blurted out "I am very short of cash, is there anything that Head Office can do to help?" "How much do you need?" he asked. I replied "Well, I urgently need at least £18,000". He held out his hand and said, "Give me your phone". I gave him my Motorola mobile, as large as house brick with an aerial on the end of it. I sat nervously waiting for someone to answer the phone. Nigel had called the managing director of our company. He said, "Hello John it's Nigel, How are you? .... Can you send a cheque for Twenty Thousand Pounds to Moray McGuffie today please, ..., great, ... thanks, ... bye". I was speechless! He smiled saying that I would receive the money the next day, which I did. It enabled me to get back on an even keel.

A manager who was part of my team at the Swansea office, which was now my base, had been trying to sell his apartment on the Swansea Marina for a long time. He was feeling quite despondent about his predicament. Without hesitating, I offered to buy his apartment and arranged a mortgage in addition to the one for my own house. My plan was to stay there instead of in hotels. Another reason was that my wife and I were growing further apart. Most evenings at home I would spend in my den, listening to and playing music or watching movies. The marriage was on a downward spiral and I didn't care that much about it. My belief was that money would solve all my problems so I worked even harder.

Nigel used to motivate us through the usual methods and also told us that financial commitment was part of being motivated. Therefore buying property with mortgages and cars on finance was the norm. I used to say exactly the same to my team too. The message was "Commit, commit, commit". I remember him telling me that "I was living in a chicken run," not long after I had bought our large luxury house. I couldn't believe it. At the time I had seven offices and about 180 people working in my region. He said, "Come on Moray, when are you going to get serious? There is girl in our Swindon office with a team of six who has just bought a large detached house and a Porsche 911". That night I was feeling fed up and thinking of a way to show him how committed I was. I didn't want to move house, as I also had the flat and shares in a property business so I decided to buy a couple more expensive cars. I didn't want someone who was well below me in rank to be seen driving a better car than me. There was no way that I was going to allow that to happen.

The next day I rang my local BMW dealer who was a neighbour of mine to order a BMW 735i for £38,000. It was metallic black with wide alloy wheels and had a leather interior. I put the phone down and then immediately rang the Porsche garage. I asked the sales person if he had any 928 S4s in stock. One was due to arrive in three to four weeks. It was white, with all the gadgets and had a blue leather interior with white piping on the seats. "How much is it?" I asked. He replied "£59,957". I said, "I'll take it".

There was a pause on the phone and I'm sure that he thought I was joking. I rang Nigel and told him that I had just spent £97,000 on cars. I was excited and couldn't wait to pick them up. The truth was that I didn't buy them; I just financed them through a couple of large car loans, which added another £2,000 a month to my already huge expenditure. I didn't really care that the cars were financed. I just wanted to pose in them and say to other people "Hey, look at me!"

At this time our son Matthew was born, I was so thrilled. We already had two beautiful girls, now a son completed the family. I stayed home for just two days and arranged for my mother in law to come to the house for a week so I could get back to work.

Sadly I didn't spend the time I should have done with my family. My focus, as always, was elsewhere. At home one room was converted into a cinema with a large screen video projector and a top quality sound system. It even looked like a cinema and I was very proud of it. As a child I used to dream of being able to show films at home on a projector. Yet another goal had been achieved in my materialistic world.

I gave my wife my BMW 735i, which was identical in every way except colour to my new black one, except it was metallic blue. I sold a six-month old XJS Jaguar with just a few thousand miles on the clock. I picked up the Porsche which broke down the very day I had it. I should have realised then that it was a bad move. I loved posing in it and very often would arrive in a car park to find people looking at the car and peering in the windows. Before leaving the car park I always revved up the engine and then sped away, looking in my mirrors at the people I was leaving behind. In addition to these was a red Porsche 911 so in total five high performance cars on my drive plus two others to run around in.

I became a real big head. I visited the local Chinese takeaway a couple of times a week and making sure to be in a different car each time. I always parked right outside the door so the customers in the takeaway could see my different cars. One member of the family who owned the takeaway came to work for me some years later. She told me "We had a nickname for you when you came to the shop". "What was that?" I asked her. She replied "Fat Wallet". It is sad to say that at the time I loved hearing it.

To our children the lifestyle we had seemed perfectly normal. One morning, when my eldest daughter Hannah was about seven years old, I took her to visit my sister. I asked her what car she wanted to go in. We went outside the house, where my four neighbours were all working in their gardens. Hannah stood still, pointed at the cars and said loudly "Eeenie meenie minie mo" and she went through the whole rhyme pointing at each car in turn. The neighbours watched in amazement, while I just smiled quietly to myself. It just served to fuel my already oversized self-image. When I look back now it seems unreal.

I couldn't wait to tell the guys in the office the next day. Having lots of money and a flashy lifestyle made me lose touch with reality, to the point that I thought that people would be motivated by hearing about how much I was earning, about my cars, holidays and the Savile Row tailor who used to visit my house. I bought twelve hand made suits, coats and blazers, some of which were quite outrageous. The truth was that boasting about these things actually had a de-motivating effect in most cases, but I did not realise that at the time. The last thing people wanted to know was how well I was doing and how much money I had. Many of the people I spoke to were struggling themselves and trying to make ends meet. I was too focused on myself to even notice.

The arguments at home continued, which made me unhappy. One evening, while I was driving on the motorway, I argued with my wife for about half an hour on my mobile phone. She lost her temper and slammed down the phone on me, which really annoyed me. I rang back and she didn't answer, so the answer phone cut in. I shouted, "Pick up the phone!" I did this three times but she still wouldn't answer. I hung up, deciding calmly that it was time to call it a day. I was away for a few days and planned to tell her our marriage was over when I got home. Breaking the news that I was leaving started a war between us that went on for years.

Chapter 10

Desperate men do desperate things ....

I moved into my apartment in Swansea Marina, chose new furniture and gradually moved my belongings from the house. I saw the children on Saturdays, usually taking them out somewhere for the day. This all went fairly well for a while. I always felt awkward around my wife so would spend as short a time as possible talking to her. After a few months she told me my youngest daughter Megan didn't want to come out with me anymore, a situation which continued for some time. I now know that in bitterness my wife had told Megan that I was going to take her away and as a result she was frightened to come out with me.

During a training course in my Cardiff office where I was instructing a group of ninety advisers, some new trainees walked past. One of them caught my attention to the point that I momentarily stopped speaking. Afterwards I found out that this stunning beauty was called Desiree. Our paths crossed several times over the next few months and finally I persuaded her to come for a meal with one of my branch managers and his girlfriend. It was only at the restaurant that Desiree realised she was accompanying me. We had a great time that night and within a few weeks we were seeing each other on a regular basis. We soon fell madly in love. Jealousy flared up in the offices, the gossip inevitably being that she was with me just because of my wealth. I did have money for about a year or so but things started to go sour. From earning £15,000 plus a month my income plummeted to nothing.

The company went through the same problems that it as it had before, but it was much worse this time. I earned hardly anything for a few months and as a result started missing the monthly payments on my cars, which amounted to £4,000. In fact I got behind with everything and had to borrow yet more money from the company. The pressure was on again. I had a disagreement with Nigel Prior, and Ron Donaldson became my manager. My region was merged with a smaller one. This had the effect of building up my income for about 8 months until it started to fall rapidly again. The Company Chairman told me that they could no longer help by loaning me money. It felt as if the nails were starting to go into the coffin. How situations can change!

Only a few months before this Ron Donaldson and I had a meeting to plan the next eighteen months and estimated that I would be earning £50,000 a month. I was 31 and believed that I would be able to retire at forty, with a pot of about £15,000,000 in the form of shares. I was totally convinced that this would happen. The reality was that not long after this the manager of my Taunton office resigned, as did a few others, due to the problems the company was experiencing. This in turn meant that I had to spend two or three days a week in the Taunton office. I now had to travel down further from Swansea; I didn't enjoy the driving and simply couldn't afford the cost of the fuel each day. Three cars returned to the finance company because I was missing payments. My Porsche 928 S4 that I had paid almost £60,000 for was sold for just £23,000 at auction. The company wanted their money back, amounting to around £80,000 for the three cars. The financial pressure was intense.

In the Taunton office I discovered Teresa, an extremely popular member of the team, was a medium who spoke to 'spirits'. One day I was talking to her and she told me information about my father and grandmother. Taken in by this she got my attention. I told a Christian acquaintance about what had happened who warned me that it was extremely dangerous to get involved with mediums because they were not talking to dead people as they believed they were. He had become very distressed about the subject during our conversation.

Around that time Desiree's grandfather died after a long illness. She was extremely close to him and naturally was devastated when he died. We had booked a holiday abroad and she didn't know whether to go away. I suggested that she spoke to Teresa who might be able to offer some comfort in view of what she had told me about my family. Desiree had a long chat with Teresa, felt comforted and decided to go on the holiday. We didn't understand what we were getting into by being involved with her in this way. I am now aware that people who believe mediums, genuinely think that they are speaking to the dead, but that is not true. It is a subject that I will not expand on now. The relationship with Teresa led us both down the wrong path. We had approached her because we desperately wanted to hear some good news. Life was so stressful at the time. Ron Donaldson used to say, "Desperate men do desperate things". He was right. I was a desperate man.

The situation continued to be very difficult with my estranged wife. I wasn't able to send money in the way I had previously and that caused her a lot of problems. However, some positive things were happening too; Megan had started to come out with me on Saturdays and Desiree was seeing the children with me.

To make myself feel better when feeling down, I usually went shopping. I bought a professional keyboard and wrote songs, which were mainly about Desiree in one way or another. One day at my Taunton office Teresa showed me a book of poems she had written. I thought that they were rather morbid as they were mainly about death and loss. I told her that if she wrote some lyrics I would try to put a tune to the words. The next day she handed me some lyrics entitled "I won't look back". When I got home I found composing the tune easy and it didn't take me long. I rang her and sang the song down the telephone. She was so impressed that she had wrote yet more. I recorded them on tape and she played them in the pubs she went to and said that people loved them. Desiree and I became increasingly involved with her because she was a very caring person and often spoke to what she said were the spirits for us. Teresa became a good friend and we spent hours talking to her on the phone in the evenings asking for guidance and advice.

Composing and playing songs was a welcome distraction from the financial pressure that I was under. Over the next few weeks I wrote more songs and recorded a few on a portable recording studio in my apartment with a neighbour who was a good guitarist. Teresa told me once that 'the spirits' had informed her I was going to be a successful songwriter and I believed her. In a few months we became dependent on speaking to her for advice on even trivial matters. I nearly started a business with her in Financial Services and a number of advisers had agreed to join us. An insurance company who said that they would invest money in the business; prospects looked good I decided to resign in order to set up the company.

I drove to Head Office to see our Managing Director, but arriving I found the chairman Michael Ravens waiting in the corridor in an extremely confrontational manner. "What are you doing here?" he asked in an aggressive tone. I replied "I have come up to hand in my resignation". "Resign!" he shouted, "You are going to leave and take some of our people with you. Let me tell you that if you do that I will sue and bleed you dry. Do you understand me?" I stood there in silence and total disbelief. He pulled me into his office and continued his verbal attack for some time. Thankfully he calmed down after a while and asked if there was any way that he could help me.

I explained my financial situation. I told him that unless things could be sorted out I faced bankruptcy. He said, "Well if you go bankrupt I will back you". He sent me to the Compliance Department to go through my situation in detail. The head of the department, someone I had known for a few years and normally a hard man with such matters, was surprisingly considerate. He put his arm around my shoulder, saying "Don't worry Moray; we will sort this out somehow". I felt relieved and informed my accountant that the Chairman said it would be okay if I declared bankruptcy. He said, "Before you do, just make sure that you definitely have his backing, because you need to be certain". I put down the phone, gathered myself together and called the Chairman. When he answered I told him that I intended to file the bankruptcy papers and asked him if he was still with me. He replied "Yes Moray, I might back you". I was speechless, and after a few moments fumbled a thank you and a goodbye. What was I going to do now? He had blocked me from starting my own business. The stress started to build up and my blood pressure increased requiring visits to my doctor.

When I visited my branch offices (16 of them) I had always been dynamic and forceful in my approach. Over the time I was in management, staff became frightened of me because I would not tolerate negativity from anyone. Now though, my life was falling apart and my managers knew something was very wrong. They could see that I had lost my spark and my edge, which caused them to complain about me. They needed and wanted a strong driven leader at a time when I had become weaker drained by the burden of the worry and pressure.

In the meantime Teresa had been in contact with a recording studio in London. We hired it for a day and went to record two songs. I don't know where the money came from, but I managed to find it from somewhere. It was fantastic doing the recordings, especially working with top musicians. The people who ran the studio were from Jamaica. We got on very well with them, especially Desiree whose late grandfather was Jamaican. It was quite hard work as we were recording until three in the morning! Having been brought up in the West Country, it was the first time I had ever encountered people who were regular drug users. Most of them smoked Ganja which seemed to relax them, but a couple of the guys took something else which made them become very loud and excitable. I didn't like it when this happened as it put me on edge.

We went back to record some more tracks. We stayed with the owner of the studio at his flat nearby as we got on well with him and had a great relationship with the musicians too. They seemed down to earth and I learnt that most of them were Buddhists. One of them gave me a book on Buddhism to read but I only scanned a couple of pages.

In the mornings the studio manager would kneel in front of a kind of shrine, tap a bell with a piece of wood and begin a strange kind of loud chanting. Desiree and I smiled at each other, as it seemed a little weird to us. I asked someone at the recording studio what he was doing and he said that if you say the chant it helps you progress and sort out your problems. "I need that", I said, as my life was just one big headache at the time.

The next week while driving to a meeting I decided to do the chant myself using the language that I was to say it in, I repeated it for a couple of minutes. I stopped abruptly because I had a strange experience that frightened me – it was as if I was watching a black and white speeded up film of my life! Profoundly shaken by this event, I decided that Buddhism was definitely not what I was looking for. *I wanted a rest from my problems but I didn't have the first idea of where to find the real peace I so badly wanted and needed.*

Financially things were getting extremely desperate and I was even further in arrears with all of my debts. The bank had started to get tough and eventually demanded their money back; it really was the beginning of the end for me. The company gave me some money that was held in shares, which we used as a deposit for another house. How we managed to get the mortgage I will never know.

Still very concerned about presenting the right image we found a property in an up market area. It was a very large four bedroom mansion with big white Roman pillars at the front. There was a very large garage and the entire loft was floored. I put all of my music equipment up there, the perfect place for my song writing. The place was far too big for just the two of us.

Around this time my old boss Mickey Rafferty contacted me asking me to join him to build his own Financial Services company. I joined because of the terms we negotiated - a £10,000 golden hello plus £7,000 a month for three months. I resigned from my company and was threatened with legal action if I tried to steal any staff from them. The money promised didn't come through as arranged and I had to ask repeatedly to get it. I managed to recruit fifty sales people in twelve weeks. Things started to go wrong with his business, people were getting unsigned cheques and so on and as a result they started leaving. Very soon we were all out of a job and it was nearly Christmas.

One of the new advisers who had joined me asked me one day if I had heard of a set of training tapes called Neuro Linguistic Programming (NLP) Selling. I had heard of NLP as a form of therapy and communication through a few success strategy books I had read. He lent the tapes to me and I enjoyed learning about this new psychological method of sales. An idea came to me - to learn to present the course parrot fashion. I decided to become a professional motivational speaker and sales trainer. I had proven myself in speaking around the country and was well known in my industry. I felt sure things could be turned around, but the trouble was I was worrying constantly, unable to sleep. I rapidly slid into depression and really needed some kind of help, but I didn't know where to look for it. Far too proud to go to my doctor, so down that I didn't even ask the God I had prayed to in the past to help me. Desiree could only watch helplessly the dynamic self-assured achiever I was, turn very quickly into the depressed worrier I had become. I was a total mess.

Starting to build up the cars, it's crazy later as I had three
different Porsches, plus Jaguars and BMWs

Starting to believe that I had arrived. A legend in
my own mind.

Ticked off my goal list. A photo in front of the
Hollywood sign.

High flying party with Desiree and a magician in California

Chapter 11

Falling....

I spent a considerable amount of time developing the Neuro Linguistics sales course. I had already done this successfully once before with the "Diamond Method". Sales people who followed it saw their production increase substantially. I enjoyed giving the training and got even more pleasure when people came and gave me feedback on the success they had from putting it into practice. I wasn't entirely sure how to market it, further complicated by the fact was that I was under enormous financial pressure.

A very good friend of mine, Chris Reading, informed me that the author of the tape set I had listened to time and time again was lecturing in London. We arranged to go along. The seminar he ran had different content to that on the tapes and gave me many more ideas. I chatted with him at lunch and he suggested ways to market my speaking, such as offering a free training session at a company's offices, then inviting them to pay a fee for a specific course. That is exactly what I did and it worked out well for a while. I opened a small office in Ammanford, Carmarthenshire above an estate agency with the limited funds available and started the business from there. Desiree had started selling dried flower arrangements, so we had a very small income, but we still couldn't pay all the bills, which were piling up every day. We planned to get married after my divorce which was taking a long time to come through.

From the outside we both appeared extremely successful, but that masked the real situation. When we started seeing each other, people had said that Desiree was only with me for my money, but nothing could have been further from the truth. I arranged a couple of courses for small groups, which went well. It was during this time that I met two brothers, Phylip and Michael Morgan, who were local businessmen. I got on well with them both, extremely well in fact. There was something different about them, but I couldn't work it out. At the time I was far too engrossed in my own situation to discover what it was. *I was to find out later on.*

One afternoon when I had just got home from the office Desiree told me that a man wearing a tee shirt and jeans had called for me. About a minute later there was a knock on the door which I opened and the man she had described standing there. He said "Mr. McGuffie?" I replied "Yes, that is correct". He pulled an envelope from behind his back and handed it to me saying, "I have got to give you this". I took it and opened it. The contents were a writ for £86,000 from the company that had financed my cars. I was shocked for a moment or two, but when I realised how he had got me to take the envelope in my hand, which meant that the writ was served, I actually shook his hand and thanked him.

The divorce came through on a Monday, Desiree and I got married on the following Saturday. Our wedding plans were subject to the decree absolute, which was delayed, we even asked the vicar if he would do a pretend ceremony, but of course declined. Obviously we couldn't afford a honeymoon, we were totally broke. We carried on struggling and became quite adept at pretending that we were fine financially. After we had been married a couple of months Desiree came into my office with some news. She was pregnant! We were both delighted, though it was difficult because we didn't have money to buy baby clothes and equipment. It was tough time, made even worse when I explained we were likely to lose our house due to our financial problems. After I left for work Desiree spent the entire day upstairs so that she didn't have to answer the door to people wanting money.

During this time I got to know Phylip and Michael very well. When I talked with them I would swear all the time which was something I had done for years. I didn't even notice that they never swore. Somehow I managed to persuade Michael to let me buy a computer and printer by instalments. I gave him six post dated cheques hoping that the money would come in to pay them. I also dropped my surname marketing myself as Moray Lawrence, convinced that it would make a difference. I developed a free training session and combined it with a short stand up comedy routine telling jokes about being stopped by the police for speeding and flying. As before, I always included jokes in my speeches, but this was different, as I felt like I was performing in a way. People would roar with laughter and the feedback from the trainees was very encouraging – these psychological techniques worked successfully for them and their sales had increased substantially.

One afternoon I had a problem with my computer and asked Michael if he could come to the house and fix it. He turned up after work and we went to the kitchen for a cup of tea. I was bending down reaching into fridge getting the milk when he said "Moray, there is something that I have got to tell you". "What's that mate?" I replied thinking he was going to ask me for more money. His answer completely stunned me, but I tried very hard not to show it. He said "Phyl and I,…. Well,… we are both born again". "Oh that's nice," I said trying to look unfazed – but my immediate thought was "Oh no, not more of those freaky Christians." My mind went straight back to when I was in Terry Ford's car. Toooooooooooooooooot! "Oh please not again" I thought. It was hard to accept because I genuinely liked the two of them. There was something about them that was different. They always seemed happy, ready to have a laugh and exchange verbal banter. *In time I would discover why they coped with life in the way they did.*

Desiree came into the kitchen and I blurted out "Mike and Phyl are born again Christians". "Are you?" she asked Mike enthusiastically. "I believe in God, I am a Roman Catholic", she said. Desiree had told me that she believed in God on a couple of occasions but I dismissed it saying I thought it was nonsense. I busied myself while they chatted to each other. I was still puzzled because they seemed to be what I thought of as normal. They certainly weren't what I imagined Christians to be like. They didn't come across as the nerdy, freaky train spotter type of people I thought Christians were. I remembered my habit of swearing when I was with them and I felt a bit guilty. That was when it dawned on me that they hadn't sworn at all, so I did my best to curb my language when with them, which was quite difficult.

The next day I visited their shop and joked as I usually did. Within a few minutes however we started talking about Jesus. Phyl became quite confrontational and talked to me about life after death, about eternity and asked what I thought would happen to me when I died. I felt under huge pressure and didn't like that. The next few times I saw them we debated the subject again. I enjoyed the discussions but I always felt under pressure. *It was during these times that I began to experience an inner conviction regarding the way that I lived my life which made me feel very uncomfortable.*

Chatting with Desiree one evening, I complained that Mike and Phyl had been putting me under pressure. She said, "Well tell them to shut up. What are you afraid of? You're a Black Belt at Karate aren't you?" I was a coward about it all and in the end I asked Desiree to tell them to stop bringing up the subject of Jesus. After she spoke to them we had no conversations about Christianity at all and amazingly that started to wind me up! When I saw them again things were just as before, we would laugh and joke, but the subject of God, Jesus or the Holy Spirit never came up. They could see that I was having financial problems, extended my credit and didn't even bank my rubber cheques.

One morning I called into the shop for a chat as I did most days. The conversation was the same as usual, but as I was just about to leave for my office Mike tossed a small, green Christian tract to me. I caught it in mid-air as he said, "You should have a read of that". I answered "I will when I get back to the office".

I looked at the cover and knew that the booklet was about God. I wanted to read it straightaway and headed back to my office. I sat down at my desk and opened the tract. In a very simple way it contained details about the Fall of Man, how Adam and Eve's sin had separated Man from God. It pointed out that there was now an impassable gap, which was illustrated by two hills with a deep valley in between them. The chasm made it totally impossible to reach God to have a personal relationship with Him. It then showed a picture of Jesus on the Cross bridging the gap so that by accepting Him as Lord and Saviour we can walk across the bridge to get to God. I didn't have any problems with that at all but the very last page of the booklet made me really angry. It said that I was living my life in rebellion to God if I wasn't following Him. For some reason, inexplicably furious, I picked up the tract and marched back to the shop ready for an argument. I still can't believe that I did it, but was very cross and said to myself indignantly "I am NOT living my life in rebellion to God!"

When I got there I told Mike that the tract was a load of rubbish. He explained exactly what it meant and reasoned with me about it. I calmed down eventually and we discussed exactly what Jesus did through His atoning death on the cross. Mike explained that Jesus died for me so that I could be with Him and have eternal life. It was a gift that I could receive by asking for forgiveness for my sin and by accepting the sacrifice that Jesus had made for me on the Cross. It made a bit more sense to me, but I couldn't understand the part about God becoming a man, knowing that He was going to be tortured and then die the death of a common criminal so that I could have eternal life. Why do that? I couldn't get my head around it, no matter how hard I tried. It still seemed like foolishness. "Why would anyone suffer like that for me?" I thought. It did interest me though and I looked forward to discussing it further, which we did many times over the following months.

Some days later I talked to Mike and explained about our friend Teresa, the medium. I told him that she spoke to 'the spirits' and that she could predict the future. I was surprised at his reaction. He became extremely serious and said that it was a very dangerous area. He said that I shouldn't get involved in anything like that because it was demonic. I said "But Mike, she can tell the future". He stared straight at me and said with total conviction "Look, I'm telling you, she couldn't tell me about my future because of my faith in Jesus Christ". It was plain to see he sincerely meant what he said and that there was no doubt in his mind at all. His reaction to what I had told him disturbed me so I decided to ring Teresa to discuss it when I got back to my office.

I hadn't spoken to her much over the previous few months because of all that was going on. I phoned her and we chatted for a few moments before I broached the subject saying "By the way I have a couple of good friends who have told me about Jesus and I am seriously considering becoming a Christian and giving my life to God". Her reaction didn't just surprise me, it shocked me. She said "Oh He wont **!!**!* help you and you will never have money again," "Why not?" I asked. "You just won't", she said. She was very nasty about it in the way that she said it. Normally Teresa was so caring and supportive, but her attitude and reaction this time was the exact opposite.

We finished the conversation and I hung up the phone. I quietly sat there bewildered for a few moments and thinking "What right does she have to say that to me?"

What she said had got to me and for the first time in my life, the penny dropped as I realised the truth - that there really was good and evil in the world.

Chapter 12

Falling into a Divine Intervention

My financial situation worsened, every day another pile of letters demanding money dropped through the letterbox. It was a horrible time; I hated answering the phone and constantly feared hearing a knock at the door. We became experts at hiding whenever the doorbell rang, stealthily moving to an area of the house where no one could see us, even if they walked around outside looking through the windows.

As the pressure increased, I became more and more depressed; at my lowest ebb even contemplating that I would be better off dead. The harder I tried to sort things out the worse it all seemed to get. I did the odd speech putting on a front, acting dynamic, charismatic and motivated, when in fact I was the complete opposite. Looking back to those times it is hard to believe that I was able to carry it off.

The more pressure created depression which was dragging me down into a bottomless spiral with no way out other than a miracle, or a win the Sun newspaper bingo, which I did without fail every day. I had spent the £40,000 winnings over and over in my head. Pay this off, do that, buy that and so on. I knew exactly where every penny would go. Sometimes I even daydreamed of finding a bag of stolen money. There seemed to be no way out of the mess. Things were very bad indeed.

One sunny summer evening, Phyl and his wife Ruth turned up at the house with a takeaway for four and a Pictionary game. Although I am not that fond of board games, the sight of a Chinese meal was enough for me. I welcomed them in and we enjoyed the food and had a good time together.

During the evening I decided to be honest with them both confiding how dire our circumstances were. Phyl had known that things were tough for us, but was taken aback to hear the awful truth in detail.

I will never forget him looking straight at me as he said, "Moray, it's simple, there is only one answer to the problem". "What is that?" I asked eagerly. He replied very definitely and with great conviction. "Ask God to sort it out for you and He will". "Oh, here we go again" I thought. I enjoyed the debates that we had over the months I had known him, but didn't believe what he said and looked at Desiree questioningly for her reaction. She believed him totally. However, I simply could not understand why God would want to get involved in a grim, desperate situation like mine. It just didn't make any sense at all.

When they left for home I pondered over Phyl's words thinking to myself, if there was a God, then He would sort out my dilemma with another highly paid job, surely? It seemed a logical solution to me, but I know now that He doesn't do things that way. I have heard stories over the years of people who have said that they have prayed asking God for a win on the Football Pools or the National Lottery, pledging to follow Him if they were to win, but I have never heard of anyone giving God credit for his or her winnings.

I thought long and hard that night. After much soul-searching I decided to say a prayer to God on my own in the kitchen. Money and needing a high paying job being my only motivation to pray, I made sure that Desiree was out of ear shot and said something like, "God, if You are real then I will believe in You". The problem was my attitude and motivation were completely wrong. I was guilty of 'Stinking Thinking" as Zig Ziglar says.

I wasn't concerned about things like eternal life, asking for forgiveness of sins, or having a personal relationship with the Lord Jesus Christ. I desperately needed money from a highly paid job, and I needed it quickly. End of story.

I continued to pray like this almost every day. For the first few weeks I prayed with the same "I need money now" attitude. However, my daily prayer gradually changed over time and I began to say it from my heart rather than just searching for an end to my money problems. Without realising it was happening, I became less focussed on my own situation and more focussed on God.

I sat up in bed with a start one Saturday morning and said to Desiree, "I want to go and buy a Bible today". She looked a little surprised but said she was fine about it. We were meeting her parents for the day and going to Cardiff. We had just £15 but decided to use it to buy a Bible. We searched through a few shops and bought a Good News Bible (because it had a few pictures in it).

That evening I started reading the book of Genesis. Over the next few days I went through the next few books, reading about Cain and Abel, Noah, Moses, Joshua and so on.

I read on through other books hoping to have some kind of a divine revelation, but nothing happened at all; no beams of light, no choirs of angels.

It just seemed to me as if I was reading stories. They were interesting stories, but nothing more, nothing less.

A few days later I popped into the shop to see Mike and Phyl as I had decided to tell them what I had done. Although Phyl appeared calm hearing my news, much later he admitted that inwardly he felt like he had just scored the winning try to win the rugby Grand Slam for Wales and in the dying seconds against England in Cardiff Millennium stadium at that!

We were completely unaware that many people were praying for us. Phyl had asked the people in his church explaining that we were in a desperate situation and needed God to intervene in a miraculous way. They had been fervently praying for weeks asking God to bring us through the problems and to realise for ourselves that God was the answer we needed.

"What have you been reading?" Phyl asked me casually. I explained that had read the book of Genesis and some of the other books at the beginning of the Bible. He suggested I read the Gospel of John in the New Testament. I asked him "Why should I read that? It's near the end of the Bible isn't it?" He grinned widely and said, "Yes, that's right. You should read it because it is all about Jesus. I know that you will find it very interesting". "Okay, I will give it a try" I replied.

Nothing to lose by taking a look I thought; so I did, but just like the book of Genesis and the others I had read, nothing really spoke to me.

However, reading the book of John did affect me and some strange things started to happen which I could not explain or understand. When watching the television or speaking to someone I often saw a verse of scripture on the television screen or hovering above the head of the person I was speaking to. It was John 3: 16:

"For God so loved the world that he gave his one and only Son, that whoever believes in him shall not perish but have eternal life" John 3:16 (NIV)

I was worried about these occurrences and didn't let on to anyone, especially not Desiree in case she wondered if I was cracking up under the strain of the circumstances. I would ask myself, "Am I losing my mind, because this certainly is not normal?"

We were really struggling for money living on a diet of chips as potatoes were cheap, but this wasn't healthy, especially for Desiree as she was pregnant.

She even got a form of lockjaw due to tension and at one point was unable to open her mouth more than half an inch. The financial pressures and the stressful consequences upon our lives caused her to grind her teeth during her sleep. Seeing her affected like this made me feel guilty and powerless; I had no idea what to do.

I did my utmost to be positive, but it was becoming increasingly difficult. I couldn't keep a happy persona and sunk ever deeper into despair. I was far too proud to try to get any normal type of job, instead wanting one that matched my capabilities and my concept of status. Seeking work was further limited because we couldn't afford a car. Not knowing what to do one day, out of sheer desperation, I suggested to Desiree that we should stay with her parents for a couple of days to get away from the pressure. We intended to stay for just the weekend, but that stretched into six weeks.

We literally had no money at all during that time and relied on my in-laws to feed us. They were struggling already as my father-in-law was recovering from a car accident that had badly injured his back and made him unable to work. Having us living there increased the pressure on them.

We slept on the sofa bed every night in the front room. I went back to our house on a couple of occasions to get clothes and other items only to find a mountain of bills behind the door. I hated going there and couldn't get out of there fast enough

I took the computer to Desiree's parents and started writing a book. I was going to call it "Goals, reasons to get into action", full of goal planning tips and how to maintain a positive mental attitude whilst working towards an objective. Unsurprisingly, I didn't finish it. My depressive mindset was most definitely not compatible with goal achieving.

Yet I knew that something was happening. My daily prayer to God each day was changing and grew in its intensity. It was less and less about money and me, and much more about asking God to help me. I still wasn't totally convinced He was real, but without a doubt I was definitely searching for Him.

At one point I considered starting to teach Karate again, knowing that it would bring in some cash fairly quickly. Unfortunately, because of the depression I wasn't in the right frame of mind to teach. I was also unfit and it would take time to get my body into condition. I needed funds immediately so I shelved the karate idea – physically and mentally it was impossible.

I did the best I could to be upbeat for Desiree's sake because it was so difficult for her. Thankfully my in-laws were very supportive to us through that dreadful time. I made the difficult decision to stop contacting my children. I didn't speak to them for several months. The reason was to avoid being asked for money by my ex-wife. I missed my children very, very much but I couldn't talk about finances. It devastated me, knowing that my failures were causing enormous difficulties for them, a painful echo from my past which I would have given anything to prevent.

We sold a few items in the local paper to raise some cash. We knew that we had to move out from Desiree's parent's home soon. I decided to do something, bite the bullet and try yet again to get out of the mess. We contacted a few estate agents to see if there were any rental properties available nearby to where we had been living.

We viewed a newly built house in an affluent area, a large detached property, which looked very impressive. It was in keeping with the image I wanted to portray so we agreed to take it. The trouble was we didn't have the £790 deposit required in order to sign the lease agreement.

Though I badly needed to get a job I was very choosy and still didn't want to get a position that was below me. Even then, in the midst of a financial horror story, I was still a legend in my own mind and in the vice-like grip of my stubborn pride. I re-established links with a few clients I had run training courses for, one in particular was very friendly and worked as a branch manager of a large financial advising company in the south of England.

He rang me one day saying he had a client, a multi millionaire, who was looking for someone to help run his business. My contact told the client about my track record. He had recommended me and asked me to ring him. Thanking him I took the number. I told Desiree this and prepared myself to make the call to him.

It would be a telephone call that would lead to an incredible life changing experience that undoubtedly was a divine intervention.

Chapter 13

The light switched on....

I rang the businessman and we had a long chat about his organisation. We hit it off really well and enjoyed discussing his business. He said enthusiastically "Right Moray, you sound just the sort of person I am looking for, do you think you can meet me tomorrow morning at my house in the Midlands? "Yes of course, no problem. Give me a time and I'll be there," I replied. In fact there was quite a big problem of course - I had no car, and no money. Desiree's father would have lent me his car, a rusty ancient Triumph Acclaim, but it would never have made it there. Since his accident Desiree's parents were struggling and short of money themselves because it had left her Dad unable to work. Despite being fully aware of the obstacles, I still agreed to a meeting time and said that I looked forward to meeting him face to face. He gave me the directions to his house.

I put down the phone and saying aloud to myself "How on earth are you going to get there?" Literally just seconds later the phone rang. It was Phyl. "Hi Moray," he said. "Hi mate" I replied, wanting to tell him about the conversation I had just had. He continued, "Look Moray, Mike and I have just had to dismiss the person that was in charge of our signage business". My immediate thoughts were, "Right... but what does that have to do with me?" He went on, "There is a fully fuelled company car here and we were wondering if you would like to use it for a few months? Just until you can get back on your feet".

As I stood there I asked myself *"Could this be God?* My reply definitely wasn't what he was expecting "Thanks! You bet I would! Can I come to church with you on Sunday"? "What?" He said in a very surprised voice. "I want to come to church on Sunday morning with Desiree" I replied. Phyl suggested "You would probably enjoy the evening meeting better as the morning service is a little more traditional". "No thanks mate, I will meet you at your house in the morning and we can go together. Afterwards you can give us dinner!" I teased. Phyl quite startled at my unexpected reaction, was nonetheless very welcoming. "Fine Moray.... I look forward to seeing you both and yes, please join us for dinner afterwards". We arranged the time to meet and I eagerly anticipated the coming weekend.

Desiree's brother Kelton drove me the 40 miles to pick up the car from them that evening. I double checked the arrangements with Phyl and Ruth for the Sunday morning and headed back to my in-laws' home. Passing the road to our house a wave of despair washed over me. Overwhelmed with such mixed emotions I took my right hand off the steering wheel, clenched my fist and raised my arm, shaking it at God and shouting at the top of my voice, "God! If You are real and You prove it to me I promise that I will follow You every day for the rest of my life!" It was a strange experience as it seemed as if I could see right through the roof of the car up to the stars above. *Boy, I really meant that prayer when I said it and now know beyond any doubt that God heard it.*

For some reason I didn't go to the meeting with the business man in the Midlands. I don't know why: perhaps it was in order to conserve the fuel that was in the car. I knew that the intended house move would require a lot of running around in the car.

We actually ended up staying at Phyl and Ruth's house the night before we went to the church. After a short drive over the mountain we arrived at the Church which was near the town of Ystradgynlais in the Swansea Valley. The church building was nothing like I had expected. It can only be described as a blue tin hut, known locally as the Band Room. Inside, about forty people were singing along to a group of musicians, a talented keyboard player, a young drummer and a woman playing an electric guitar. Phyl set up his bass guitar and joined in. They played well together and the modern music appealed to me.

I was very surprised that when the music stopped between each song that many of the people carried on singing with their hands in the air. I remembered a 'Songs of Praise', television programme that I had seen years before in which people were singing in the same way. Terry Ford's car quickly came back to mind a Tooooooooooooooooooot! The old uncomfortable feelings about Christians returned. What could I do though? The weather was horrible outside and we had come in Phyl's car, so I was stuck there. The people around me seemed to be really enjoying the singing and it was obvious that they believed in the words of the songs. (I realise now that it was because they were singing from experience and a personal knowledge of God). I didn't sing a single note, and neither did Desiree. I remember that throughout the worship I just stood there with my arms tightly folded across my chest in a very defensive posture. After some time the singing ended and everyone took their seats while some people continued to pray.

At this point a young man, who was sat behind us at the back of the hall said in a loud voice, "Jesus, Jesus, Jesus!" It surprised me because he said it with the same tone I used to tell Desiree that I loved her. His words pierced my heart and I recalled the many times that I taken Jesus' name in vain. In that instant I felt deeply convicted of the many wrong doings throughout my life. Another young man got up from his chair and gave the sermon, as the Pastor was away that day. I can't remember a word of what he said, or even what the subject of the message was. The meeting finished and we spoke to a few people who were very loving and kind. As we went back to Phyl's car he asked me what I thought of the meeting. I said it was okay but at times it seemed strange. It was not like anything I had ever experienced before. We had dinner and later Phyl's father in law Eifion, who was an Elder in the Church, turned up. We sat and talked for a while and I asked a lot of questions. He gave me simple answers to each one, helping me to understand their faith and church life, but wasn't pushy about it.

Phyl had told some of his friends at the church that I was selling items to raise cash. These included a new, hardly used video camera. Someone from the church called Martin phoned that afternoon at asking about the cameras specifications. He told me to bring it with me the following Sunday offering me the full £300 I was asking for it. This meant I would have to go back to another church meeting. When we had finished our conversation, Desiree wanted to know who had phoned. I told her a lie, saying the man who wanted to buy the camera had asked to see me that same evening so we would have to go to the church for the 6pm meeting. There were far more people in the little hall than had been in the morning service. Everyone seemed genuinely pleased to see us again and gave us a warm welcome.

The music started and this time I joined in with the singing straight away. I quickly realised that I was even singing out loud and in harmony. We sang a few lively choruses, finishing with a song called "Lord I lift Your Name on high". The lyrics struck a deep chord inside me. As we sang it together, something inexplicable happened for as I was happily singing the words: -

> Lord, I lift Your name on high,
> Lord, I love to sing Your praises,
> I'm so glad You're in my life,
> I'm so glad You came to save us.

> You came from heaven to earth to show the way,
> From the earth to the cross, my debt to pay,
> From the cross to the grave, from the grave to the sky
> Lord I lift Your name on high.

Suddenly I realised that I was singing wholeheartedly but even more significantly, actually believed the words that were coming out of my mouth! It was as if someone had switched a light on inside my head as it dawned on me – I knew, beyond any shadow of doubt that Jesus was Real! In that moment all of the resentments and negative thoughts I'd had concerning Christians were instantly wiped away. *It was amazing. I had never experienced anything like this before.*

I stood there thinking, "Wow! All this stuff about Jesus is true!" It was like the old reggae song says, "I can see clearly now". I knew in those moments that Jesus had died for me and that He was alive and in Heaven. Despite all the difficulties in my life I had a huge sense of joy in my heart. The rest of the service was a bit of a blur. I didn't tell anyone what had happened in the meeting but left the church feeling very different. I had an inner certainty of both hope and a future. I drove back to Desiree's parents' house that evening with what I can only describe as a warm glow inside of me. I could literally feel the darkness that had surrounded me disappear.

On the Monday morning I called Phyl and when I told him that I had decided to make Jesus the Lord of my life he was ecstatic! Desiree and her mum both overheard what I had said in our conversation. Her mum was very encouraging, being a member of the Catholic Church, but Desiree didn't say anything for a moment, letting the news sink in. Then she asked me guardedly, "So you've become a Christian then"? "Yes" I replied with great enthusiasm. She just looked at me as if I was from another planet.

Over the next couple of days I read a terrific book that Phyl gave called "Run baby run" by Nicky Cruz. I rang Phyl saying we would be back at church the next Sunday morning. He asked "So Moray, you are really serious about this then?" "Of course mate. You know that I am an all or nothing kind of guy" I replied. He knew I meant what I said and was very excited about seeing us at church.

We decided to go back to our own house to begin the moving out process. We made arrangements to do this at night to spare answering awkward questions which would have been embarrassing. When we arrived there at around tea time our neighbours, Gareth and his wife Sian were both working in their garden. We had got on very well with them whilst living there. We used to chat with them over the garden fence, shared meals sometimes and enjoyed a drink together at the local pub. We were both delighted when they said that they would come to our wedding.

Gareth was mowing his lawn when he saw us pull up on the drive. He came straight over asking, "How are you Moray? We haven't seen you for a while. We have been worried about Desiree and the baby. Come in for a cup of coffee". I didn't want to accept his invitation, but Desiree had already started walking across to their house. Gareth, Sian and Desiree were in the kitchen and as I walked through the hallway towards them Gareth asked with sincere concern in his voice "What's been happening Moray?" I was about to explain our predicament but the words that came out of my mouth took me by surprise as I blurted out emotionally. "I've found Jesus!" Startled, they looked first at me and then each other. I continued "I have asked Him to come into my heart and I have made Him the Lord of my life. I am born again". They continued to stare at me for a few more moments then both turned to look at Desiree. As they did she declared firmly, "I'm not, I'm still normal!" She looked completely embarrassed by my tearful acknowledgement of Jesus.

I didn't realise until that moment how I had been radically changed. My constant swearing had stopped overnight; it was as if the words had been completely erased from my vocabulary. My despair about our finances remained, but at the same time I was joyful in Jesus. It is very hard to explain these feelings, but they were totally undeniable.

I started to read the Bible avidly and soon it made more sense to me. Whereas before I couldn't understand most of what I read in it, I had now met with the Author and He was living in my heart. It was no longer just another book to me.

In order to move, we needed a deposit for the house in Ammanford. We had managed to raise £300 towards it and there was only a week to go before the moving day. We placed adverts to sell items in the local papers. We had worked out that we needed £900 for the deposit, for food and other items. The very day we went to sign we had the exact amount of money we needed so we could move in! It was amazing. We moved during the night with lots of helpers in vans with a horsebox. Phyl, his wife Ruth and Mike were a great help. Gareth, our previous neighbour, lent us a hand too. Desiree was shattered because she was heavily pregnant at the time. It was the beginning of November when we moved and very cold.

During the next few months we survived by selling all we could in the free sections of newspapers and somehow managed to get through. I was full of joy that I had given my life to Jesus, but my problems had not disappeared and still needed to be faced. The mental battle persisted, I struggled wretchedly some days with grave worries and suffered many sleepless nights. The first Sunday after moving into the house we went to church. Desiree always went with me 'as a good wife' (her words). When we came home after the morning service, parked the car on the drive and I went into the house carrying my Bible under my arm. After a minute or two there was a knock at the door.

I opened it to find our new neighbour standing smiling broadly. "Hello, my name is Geraint Morse, I am the vicar of the local Baptist church and I live next door. Why don't you pop over to meet my wife Tina and have a cup of tea with us?" I said we would be over to see them shortly. I shut the door and thought how amazing God was. *Fancy us ending up living next to a minister of the Gospel.*

We went round and met Geraint, Tina and their two boys and had a lovely time with them. I was full of it and couldn't stop talking about the Lord and recent events. I spoke about our church and ended sharing my story of how I accepted Jesus. They sat there and listened intently and were both very encouraging. They asked Desiree whether she had accepted the Lord and she told them that she believed in God and that she was a Catholic.

We spent a lot of time with them over the next few months. We had no washing machine so Tina used to do all of our laundry. We also ate there quite often which was a big help. They are wonderful Christians who let the love of Jesus flood out of them in practical ways. We thank God for them both. Geraint invited us to go to their house once a week to do a simple Bible Study with them. During those weeks we learned a lot about the Gospel. I was eager to know more about the Bible and Desiree started to think more seriously about her faith and Jesus. Every night before I went to sleep I prayed quietly "Lord, please save Desiree," and "Please remove this noose from around my neck," referring to my financial situation. I would often lay in bed and whisper prayers while she slept. December 25th that year was fantastic in a lot of ways. Christmas morning there were only a couple presents as we had very little money.

I had a box of cereal from Desiree's' younger brother JP that he wrapped up for me. It was so different to the big piles of presents that I had been used to. It snowed heavily at night on Christmas Eve and when I got up on Christmas Morning the view was like a picture postcard outside. The easiest thing would have been not to go to church because the road was covered in snow, but I told myself that we must go.

My mother was staying with us at the time so we all went along. It was a slow drive in the wintry conditions but well worth it as it was a very special service, one I'll never forget. We went home had a lovely dinner with our neighbours and spent the afternoon singing carols around the piano. I was a little embarrassed because I had never done anything like that before and would have previously avoided any activities like that. *Allowing God into my life had changed me so dramatically it was hard to recognise myself.*

Chapter 14

The Lord of Miracles

Every Sunday Desiree came to church with me, as well as to the midweek House Group meetings. She didn't say much about what was happening in her own spiritual life. I read the Bible eagerly because I wanted to understand more as quickly as possible. Desiree usually busied herself around the house even while she was heavily pregnant. We were still under considerable stress because I still wasn't working, so each day was a matter of survival.

Quite often we arrived home to find bags of shopping on the doorstep and sometimes money had been put through the letterbox anonymously, which was a great help. When we went to church my Pastor and his wife, along with others, gave us bags full of shopping. It was difficult for me to accept this charity sometimes because of my pride, but we were both very grateful indeed.

At a House Group meeting Desiree got into a conversation with Phyl's wife Ruth. They were discussing the subject of Heaven when Ruth asked her a question, "If you died today how do you know that you would get into Heaven?" Desiree replied "I would because I have been a good girl". The very moment she said that, deep down inside she felt a huge pang of guilt, remembering things she had done, knowing they were wrong. Like all people, no matter how good we are we will never be good enough to get to Heaven by our own good works - as, **"All have sinned and fallen short of the glory of God" (Romans 3:23 NIV).**

Ruth suggested that Desiree pray, asking God to show her the truth about her thoughts regarding the way of getting to heaven; or whether what I had done by accepting Jesus, asking for forgiveness for wrongdoings in her life, was the correct way. That is exactly what she did, that night and for the next few days. She was very concerned because she heard me say that since I had accepted the Lord Jesus as my Saviour I was completely assured of going to Heaven. Desiree wanted to understand why the Bible said asking God for forgiveness was important. She needed to feel certain that when she died that she would be in heaven. These issues were a challenge, because as a result of me coming to Christ and her conversation with Ruth, everything Desiree had believed all through her life was now called into question. When she prayed asking God which was the right way she truly meant it with all of her being. Desiree kept telling herself, "If Moray is going to go to Heaven I want to make sure that I will too".

One Saturday Desiree was going to visit her parents for the day while I stayed at home. I had been lent some worship tapes, which she had heard playing in the house and asked if she could have one to listen to on her journey. I gave her the first one to hand and thought nothing more of it. She arrived home late that afternoon with a glow on her face and she said "I was listening to the worship tape in the car and the song was 'Only by Grace can you enter'. I was singing along with the song and I realised that my hand was on my heart and that what I was singing was real to me". The song has always been very special to us both, and of course especially to Desiree.

Only by grace can we enter
Only by grace can we stand
Not by our human endeavour
But by the blood of the Lamb

Into Your presence You call us
Call us to come
Into Your presence You draw us
And now by Your grace we come
Now by Your grace we come

Lord, if You mark our transgressions
Who would stand?
But thanks to Your grace
We are cleansed by the blood of the Lamb

"Hang on there" I said, dashing out of the door and jumping over the garden wall, banging impatiently on Geraint's door. As the door opened I said, "Geraint, Desiree is ready to accept the Lord!" I explained quickly what Desiree said had happened in the car. Geraint's face lit up as he said to bring her over right away. The three of us sat in his kitchen while Geraint showed Desiree specific verses in the Bible.

Leafing through his bible he came to this scripture:-

"The word is near you; it is in your mouth and in your heart," that is, the word of faith we are proclaiming: That if you confess with your mouth, "Jesus is Lord," and believe in your heart that God raised him from the dead, you will be saved. For it is with your heart that you believe and are justified, and it is with your mouth that you confess and are saved." (Romans 10: 8-10 NIV)

He asked "Do you believe that Desiree"? "Yes!" she replied tearfully. Overjoyed to hear this wonderful answer to my prayers my eyes filled up too. It was an incredibly precious moment for us all. Geraint asked Desiree to repeat a prayer after him, which was something like this: "Heavenly Father, I know that I am a sinner. I know that I deserve the consequences of my sin. However, I am trusting in you Jesus Christ as my Saviour. I believe that His death and resurrection provided for my forgiveness. I trust in Jesus and Jesus alone as my personal Lord and Saviour. Thank you Lord, for saving me and forgiving me! Amen!" What a day! I thanked God for answering my prayers.

God had proved once again that He is faithful. There was a significant change in Desiree. She wanted to put things right and apologised for wrong doings from the past. One afternoon I heard her on the phone to her mother apologising for an argument they once had over her mum scorching her petticoat with an iron. Her mother was rather surprised and could tell that something had happened to her. She wondered if Desiree had made the same commitment as me, but wanted to wait until she saw her face to face to know for sure.

My financial situation was still a major cause of concern despite my joy in becoming a Christian. In our spare room there were boxes of paperwork and accounts piled up everywhere. I loathed going in there because the sight of them troubled me so much. One morning I got up and decided to burn the whole lot, reasoning that destroying them the problems go away. Carrying the stacks of boxes and files into the garden I built a bonfire, poured petrol over it and set it alight. Within a short time only a heap of ashes remained, but I felt no better. I actually felt worse because nothing had changed, the problems still had to be dealt with.

I had called into Phyl and Mike's shop one day and was having a chat with them when a plain clothes policeman came in, asking if they knew where he could find Moray McGuffie or Moray Lawrence. I had decided to use the latter – Lawrence - on all my publicity material for the courses I ran. As soon as I heard my name mentioned I slipped out of the back door and drove home, feeling very afraid. Desiree burst into tears when I told her the police were after me. Scared, I rang Phyl and Mike to discover what had happened after my sharp exit. The policeman said he was investigating complaints about training fees I should have refunded when I had cancelled a course. This was true, but had not been an attempt to defraud the clients. The police were concerned that because I was using two names I might have been a confidence trickster, which was not the case. The money for the cancelled course I had foolishly spent though aware that do so was totally wrong. Panicking Phyl said that he hadn't seen me and the policeman left the premises. However, immediately his conscience pricked him over his answer, so Phyl ran after the officer. He explained that I was now a changed man and committed my life to Christ. He continued to say our circumstances had resulted in me taking desperate measures. The policeman asked him to pass on a message, for me to phone him at the station. Before doing so I rang my solicitor to explain what had happened. He advised me this was a serious matter and it was very likely I'd be charge with the offence. "They will probably want to do you for that," he explained. My heart sunk at this. He said that if I was asked to go to the police station I should ring him first, so he would send a brief to be present when I gave a statement. This conversation made me even more frightened.

I plucked up the courage to phone the police station and was put through to the officer concerned. I said, "Hello, this is Moray McGuffie. I have been asked to call you as you have been looking for me". "That's right Sir". He said, "I need to see you, but I am going to Norwich tomorrow to collect a prisoner, so can you ring me again on Friday?" I promised I would. The rest of that day and the next seemed to pass very slowly indeed. I prayed a lot during that time and asked Phyl and Mike to do the same. On the Friday morning I rang to speak to the policeman was told he had been delayed and to ring again after the weekend

We had a night of prayer that Friday evening, which meant a group of us prayed together from 10pm till 2am at my Pastors house. During the session pastor asked if anybody needed specific prayer. I asked if they could pray for my very difficult circumstances and that God would act by Monday morning. The group prayed for me. I didn't go into detail but explained that I needed God to move in what was a desperate situation.

On the following Monday morning I called the police station and was put straight through to the officer. He thanked me for calling saying "I got back later from Norwich than expected. Look, Mr McGuffie, just forget about the complaint. If another one comes in I will contact you. I understand the situation so let's just leave it there". "Thank you" I replied, completely stunned and put down the phone. I stood in silence for a few moments still trying to take in what he had just said. *Then I broke into praise and thanked God for His intervention. It was really eleventh hour stuff.*

Desiree was well overdue for the birth of our baby and very fed up with the prolonged wait. She was also suffering from Pre-eclampsia which meant she was in and out of hospital for checks. Our fuel money soon ran out, so I rang Phyl to ask if he could put £10 of petrol in the tank. It was enough to get me to and from the hospital three or four times that week, a round trip of forty miles each time, plus other urgent errands. Labour took over thirty six hours and ended with Desiree undergoing an emergency Caesarean Section as the Doctor had discovered a serious problem. While Doctors operated I sat next to Desiree and prayed continually. I really felt the presence of God in the theatre. We were both exhausted when our beautiful daughter Bethan was finally delivered.

Visiting Desiree in hospital one morning she drew my attention to a scripture she had read saying, "When I read this scripture, I immediately thought about you": -

"If anyone does not provide for his relatives, and especially for his immediate family, he has denied the faith and is worse than an unbeliever" (1 Timothy 5:8 NIV)

As I read it, those words felt like an arrow through my heart. I hadn't been able to send money to my ex-wife and had not made contact with her or our children for a while. Desiree had an envelope and we found a white paper bag, which was about six inches by four inches. I wrote a letter to my ex wife and our children on it, by carefully tearing the bag open and laying it out flat. In the letter I apologised for my behaviour and explained how I had accepted Jesus as my Lord and Saviour. The letters I had back a few days later were wonderful. I even had one from my ex wife's best friend, which was very encouraging. The result of this was that I was able to see my children again.

I have learned over the years that sometimes when reading the Bible a verse or passage will seem to 'leap off the page'. Sometimes it can bring conviction like the verse in Timothy, sometimes comfort and sometimes a challenge. Over the years I believe that the Lord has spoken to me many times through the Bible. It really is true that the Word of God is a living word and it certainly has been to me on many occasions.

The day that Desiree and Bethan were due to come home I arrived at the hospital with the pointer of the fuel gauge resting at the very bottom, it was completely empty. I had been short of money a couple of times before and the engine had stopped with the pointer showing a higher reading than it was then. When we got into the car to leave the hospital I prayed asking God for travelling mercies and to let whatever was in the fuel tank to be enough to get us home. I drove steadily and quietly prayed for the whole of the journey. If we had broken down I had no money for fuel nor a mobile phone to call someone in an emergency. *By a miracle we got home and I praised God and thanked Him for what must have been supernatural provision. I am sure that there were Angels pushing the car as we went along.*

The Lord continued to provide and move in many ways including a major miracle when Desiree's father rang to say "Moray I have a large envelope here that has been sent to you by the court". My heart sank and I said "Go on, open the letter and tell me what it says". He read "On the 4th of March 1994 you were declared bankrupt". I stood motionless wondering what to say. He said he would bring the envelope up the next day, as there was a lot of information inside. When he arrived I read through the letter and then the big brochure, which explained what everything meant.

The next day when has handed the brochure I happened to open at the section which said destroying accounts was against the law and if convicted a person was liable to imprisonment. My mind went back to the big fire in my garden when I had destroyed everything. "I am going to be in for it now", I thought.

I made an appointment with the official receiver in Swansea. Before going I felt afraid and prayed fervently, asking God to reassure me that He would be with me at the meeting. Opening my Bible to the book of Isaiah, my eyes fell on these words, answering the cry from my heart.

"So do not fear, for I am with you; do not be dismayed, for I am your God. I will strengthen you and help you; I will uphold you with my righteous right hand" (Isaiah 41:10 NIV)

"Thank you Lord" I whispered. Geraint next door prayed with me before I left. I went into the office block with a single envelope containing just a few receipts. I continued to pray as I went up to the eighth floor in the lift. I introduced myself to the receptionist and then sat down in the waiting area quietly praying under my breath. A smartly dressed lady came to the door and asked me to come into her office. I followed her along a corridor, stepping around piles of boxes that seemed to litter our path. Curious, I asked what they contained. She explained that the boxes were filled with documents – the accounts from people and businesses that had gone bankrupt. I was there with just an envelope containing a few credit card receipts that my solicitor had held for me.

We sat down in her office and she said "Thank you for coming in, we have been trying to find you for some time. Have you been on the run?" she asked me. "Yes" I replied nervously. She continued "We have been trying to find your garage. We looked in Yellow Pages and made enquiries with motoring organisations but can't find details of it anywhere". I said, "I am sorry. I don't understand what you mean?" She said, "The garage where you have been running a car sales business". I answered "There must be some mistake, I have never been in the Motor Trade, my business was Financial Services". She looked very puzzled, held up a large file of paper and asked "Then who owned all of these cars?" Looking at the list it contained many of the high performance cars that I had financed over the years. From memory they were Porches, Jaguars, and BMWs. "They were all mine" I replied. She looked at the file in her hand and then in amazement at me. "What, all of these cars were yours?" she asked me disbelievingly. "Yes" I replied feeling very embarrassed. She shook her head in astonishment, staring at the list; then looked at me very closely as if she was trying to work me out.

She asked, "Do you have any bank accounts?" I showed her my cash point card for my only account that had £1.36 in it.

She handed me a pair of scissors and asked me to cut it in half. "Right I need to find out about your debts. Where are your accounts and paperwork?" she asked. I handed her my envelope and said, "This is all I have". She took out the contents to find a few credit card receipts and bills. I said, "Can I say that I am very glad to be here". Incredulously she asked, "Why do you say that?" For the next ten minutes she sat there in silence as I recounted the story of how I had climbed to the top of the ladder of success only to fall to the very bottom. Openly I confessed about my unpleasant aggressive attitude to my staff and how I had focused selfishly on myself. I confided how we had been encouraged to commit ourselves financially to motivate us to work harder, and how dreadful I felt when my income dried up; about the times when I couldn't open the mail, answer the door or the telephone because of the enormous fear that gripped me. How, in the end, in great despair, I even contemplated ending it all.

My eyes started to fill with tears as I told her that someone had told me about Jesus Christ. I explained why He died for me on the Cross of Calvary and how, after a period of time I received Him as Lord and Saviour of my life. The result being that instantly I was completely transformed and wanted to live my life for Him. When I finished she gazed intently at me, as if she as if she was still trying to work out if I was a crackpot. She carried on examined each bill asking me a number of questions as she filled in the required details on a large form.

When she had finished I signed it. She was quiet as she sat behind her desk considering my situation. Finally she said "Right Mr. McGuffie, you can put all of this behind you and forget about it. I am satisfied with the explanations you have given me regarding your affairs. My recommendation is that no further action be taken. You can go". I thanked her, we shook hands and I left the office. I got into the lift and raised my hands in praise to God once again. *"You are amazing Lord, thank you" I said in gratitude. I couldn't wait to get home to tell Desiree the news.*

I was at home in prayer one morning and felt God was directing me to move nearer the Church. We were living about twenty miles away and by now I had returned the car to Phyl. We managed to find a small house in the village where the church was and so we moved. We were helped a great deal during this time by Paul the man who said "Jesus, Jesus, Jesus" so adoringly that first time we went to church. He would leave his car with us if he was away, often turned up with a Chinese or Indian take-away to share; blessing us in caring, thoughtful ways we really appreciated. Paul worked for the Teen Challenge Charity, a Christian Drug Rehabilitation Centre; collecting money from boxes in shops. Sometimes I went collecting the money with him to earn a few pounds. We always had a great time with him and he taught me a lot about the Bible in those days. He was generous, just like his parents who were very kind-hearted. They invited us to a Sunday dinner each week for a few months when we had very little money. His mother was wonderful to us in those early days. A faithful Christian lady who now has gone to be with the Lord.

A few weeks after we moved into the house my Pastor and his wife came round to see us. They talked to us about lots of things and at the end of our chat the pastor said we should not allow the devil to get his hooks in us. By that he basically meant that we should live our lives honourably. When they left Desiree and I looked at the television in the corner of the room, a rental set which I had not made any payments for in a very long time. We had moved so many times that we had completely forgotten about it. We decided to take it back to the rental firm's Head Office, which was in Swansea, the next day. We prayed before we left once again asking the Lord to intervene in the situation. We wanted to arrange a repayment plan to pay what we owed. We asked for the manager and explained to him that we were returning the TV. In his office I shared my testimony recounting what had happened over the last year or so, how we both had accepted Jesus as our Lord and Saviour and how He had changed our lives for the better.

The manager motioned us over to computer at the back of his office. He brought up our details and wrote 'cancelled' on the screen. "Okay you can go home and forget about this, thank you for your honesty", he said. He even offered me a job collecting money from slot televisions. I thanked him very much was still too proud to accept. It was an area of my life that continued to be a problem, one which I needed to hand over to God to deal with.

We sat in our car, the rusty old Triumph Acclaim given to us by Desiree's' father. Amazed once again for answered prayer, we praised and thanked God for His provision.

Chapter 15

More Miracles, Revivals and Outpourings

There is no doubt that the Lord has moved many times in both life own and Desiree's. When people ask me how I know there is a God, my reply is that He has worked so many times in miraculous ways there is no doubt that He is real. I can't prove to you that God exists - the only way to find out for yourself is to experience Him in your own life. I can guarantee that He will reveal Himself to you if you ask Him.

It was a very big day for me when I went in to sign on at the Unemployment Benefit Office, completing the paperwork made me feel terribly ashamed. A couple of years before I was staying in Hollywood, living the high life, earning big money and now I was at rock bottom. It was raining hard and I hid myself under my umbrella so that no one could see me go into the Job Centre. There was no option; I was still out of work. We had managed to sell a lot of items to survive but we couldn't carry on doing that forever. I even rented a shop for a few pounds a week and sold off my extensive video collection of which I had hundreds. I managed to buy and sell some as well, which kept us going for a few more weeks. In that time I shared my story of Salvation and explained the Gospel many times with customers. It was a great training ground for me as an evangelist. I had to find work somewhere and did a few short term jobs, all of them in Sales. I sold stationery, trade association membership, security services and advertising.

My stubborn pride remained a problem; I still thought too highly of myself. We had managed to buy an old Ford Escort, which was rusty but at least it provided transport. I was travelling home from an appointment late one afternoon and pulled up at some traffic lights. While stationary, I glanced into my rear view mirror; horrified I could only watch as a car containing two young lads drove at speed towards me. They were looking at each other, conversing and not concentrating on the road. They were unable to stop in time and crashed into the back of my car. I don't know if it was training from Martial Arts, but in that split second I moved forward on the seat and braced myself for the impact. I yelled at the top of my voice as they hit the car. I tightly gripped the steering wheel and bent it into a kind of figure eight on impact. The car was a write off. This was very bad news as no car meant I would lose my job but thankfully I was able to get a new hire car from the insurance company for a few weeks as the driver admitted liability.

I was working on commission and decided to try to find a job that was salaried. There was an advert in the local newspaper for a sales person for an American industrial sales company doing business to business sales. I rang up and got an interview. When I told the person on the phone my track record he was very impressed. I was offered the job after just a few minutes of meeting him. The annual salary was £6,500 a year plus commission with a small fuel allowance. It was hard to accept because not that long before, I would have earned that amount in a week. At my interview he told me that if I proved myself they would put me into management. I phoned my Pastor and arranged to discuss it with him. After our chat I accepted the offer. I attended a training course in Colchester and was well ahead in sales skills compared to all the other attendees; my past experience in the sales industry and in training hundreds of people in the art of selling myself put me in a strong position.

Straightaway my work produced good results and within a couple of months I was promoted to supervisor. The insurance company paid out on the old Ford Escort, so we bought a cheap Renault 25, which went well until the engine broke down. The damage would have cost far too much to repair and so the car was scrapped. My boss said if I was without transport he would have to lay me off.

That night Desiree and I prayed together and she said she felt a strong word from the Lord that we should praise Him and dance before Him in thanks that He would provide us with a solution to the problem. We turned on the stereo, played a Worship CD and danced as energetically as we could. Desiree lasted for about thirty seconds and then fell on the floor laughing, as I am not the greatest dancer. I carried on for about ten minutes. Nothing happened, there was no divine revelation, no word from God in my heart. We finished our prayers and went to bed. Early the next morning I had a phone call from a friend at our church who had heard of our situation. They were a one-income family like us. When they learned about the car being scrapped, they prayed about it. They felt that the Lord told them to give me £500 to buy another car. I was very humbled when they told me. I ran upstairs to tell Desiree how God had intervened once again. *We praised the Lord there and then. We were so grateful for their obedience to the prompting of the Holy Spirit.*

We received the money and purchased a car that enabled me to get to work. Within another few months I was promoted three times, was given a new company car and a much higher salary. Then to top it all, I was asked to run the sales training courses for the company. *God is so good!*

Over the years the Lord has impressed upon us to help people who have been in need. It has been wonderful to be able to do it. I certainly believe it is better to give than to receive. We have found after giving with a cheerful heart the Lord blesses in return, very often much more than was given in the first place. A good example occurred while I was earning a low income doing the sales job. I went to a church in Newport to hear a speaker who was over from America. I remember that I had just over £2 in my pocket. I went straight to the meeting without eating and planned to use the money to buy some food on the way home. During the meeting the offering bowl was passed around. I felt the money in my pocket. Though this money was for food, as the bowl passed me by I put in £1 saying quietly, "Lord, it's not much but I am giving it to you in faith." I told no one about it including Desiree. At our next Sunday morning service my Pastor handed me an envelope which had this message written on the front of it "Told to give this to you by the Lord". I opened it later to find £100. I rejoiced and remembered the verse: -

"Give, and it will be given to you. A good measure, pressed down, shaken together and running over, will be poured into your lap. For with the measure you use, it will be measured to you." (Luke 6:38 NIV) God is amazing in the way He provides.

The prayer times Desiree and I had (and still do) became a very important part of our daily routines. One evening we were sat together on the sofa praying. We both had our eyes closed as we spoke to the Lord. I suddenly had a strong feeling that Jesus was standing before us with His hand on our heads, as if He was praying for us. The vision was very clear in my mind and I can still recall it vividly now. The presence of the Lord in the room was very powerful and I remember going ice cold when I saw this. When we stopped praying we said in unison "You will never guess what I just saw!" We had seen the vision identically in every detail: we both saw Jesus with His hands stretched out on top of our heads as we prayed. It was an incredible experience.

In my job I gave a speech on two occasions with the owner of the company from America in attendance at the meeting. The first time I was a sales person and had only been with the company for a month. He sought me out during a break and told me how much he had enjoyed what I had said. It was a good company to work for, but I discovered that my boss was an alcoholic, which made things very difficult. I had been promised another promotion, with a much bigger salary but it never happened. I learned that my manager was expecting a promotion himself, but which didn't come to fruition. Instead of telling me this, whenever I questioned him about promotion he tried to sweep it under the carpet. I would bring it up every time we met which became an irritation to him. I told him one day the Bible says, **"Hope deferred makes the heart sick"**. I said that if it was not going to happen to let me know and not to keep on avoiding it. He didn't like me speaking to him so directly, it angered him; but I had to say this because situation was causing me tremendous frustration.

The next time I gave a speech the owner was over from America again. Once again he came to tell me afterwards how much he enjoyed what I said. This time it was in front of my manager who didn't like it at all. The owner asked for my phone number, saying he would call me when he got back to America. The next day I had a call from my boss who told me that I wasn't going to get his job. He said, "You think you have made it now because the owner has got your number!" The reality was that after that speech I became a marked man and started to look around for something else. My working relationship with my boss deteriorated, becoming difficult and unpleasant. I felt that I should resign from the company. A local businessman, Robert Rees whom I had worked with some years previously, heard that I was looking for another job invited me to meet him to discuss a job offer.

On the way I prayed. I knew that the job involved sales and would be likely to include a company car. When I worked for him previously I had the use of a small Ford Fiesta van. We now had had two children at home now as my daughter Megan had come to live with us because she had seen the change in me. I prayed, "Lord if this is the right job for me, please would you let the car be a white Peugeot 406". I had seen one in a supermarket car park and liked the look of it, had absolutely no idea of what car was available. At the interview we chatted for a while and I was offered a position. Rob said, "Oh, by the way, you get a company car with the job, it's in the car park". "Great" I replied. He then said, "Have a look at it on your way out. It's a white Peugeot 406". *Could it have been a complete coincidence? I don't think it was. I prayed about the job and had a peace in my heart, so I took it.*

The sales I made for the company were steady but not outstanding to begin with. All I was doing was covering the costs for the company. Over lunch one day Rob said that I needed to bring in more sales as he was interested in profit for his business, which was a fair point to make. He wasn't running the company as a charity for me. I tried hard for the next few weeks but did not make much progress, which was unusual as in the past I had found making sales so easy. I considered leaving, perhaps going back to the American Company that I worked for before as the management staff had been replaced. The new Director of the operation in Europe had contacted me and wanted me to return.

I sat in my living room early one morning, praying, before heading off for work. I had a Christian TV programme playing quietly in the corner of the room. At the end of my prayer I said to the Lord. "Please tell me Lord whether I should remain or leave my job. I need to know quickly". I opened my eyes and there was a man with his Bible open in his hand. He pointed at the camera, which was basically directly at me and said, "The Lord is saying stay there and I will bless you" and with that the programme ended. I sat there for a moment and thought that it was a coincidence. But I said to the Lord "If that is you Lord, I receive your Word".

On the way to work, I was convicted that it was God who had spoken to me and I decided to act upon it. As a step of faith I went into Rob's office and said, "Look, I have been considering leaving for a while and I have been praying about it". I had witnessed to Robert many times up to that point, and he used to look at me as if I had gone mad (he still does whenever we meet). I think what I said next really convinced him that I had lost it. I continued and told him what had happened on the TV at the end of my prayer. I finished by saying, "I am going to prove God to you in this and He is going to bless your business with sales". Rob's expression was one of incredulity – he probably thought I was completely insane. I heard him laughing as he told his father about our conversation. I had nailed my colours to the mast. *If God had spoken, it would happen.*

That week ten sales came in over the phone from companies I had called on but who had given us no business whatsoever up until then. These sales more than doubled my turnover. Within a couple of months I was generating over a third of the company's entire turnover. The business went through a period of massive growth and success. I still believe that it was because of what the Lord said and not because of me. I have reminded Rob about it over the years as we still keep in touch.

During this period a Revival broke out in a church in Pensacola, Florida. Some of our church leaders went to visit and came back with amazing stories of how God was moving. People were lining up at the church door from 7am in the morning just to get into the evening meetings! We had heard that people were giving their lives to Jesus every night at the Revival gatherings and were running to the altars to repent. There were healings and miracles taking place almost daily. I heard stories of school students who had been to the Revival saying grace in the dinner hall at college and the power of God falling on the room, students realising their sinfulness, were repenting and giving their lives to Christ. I wanted to go to Pensacola but the cost was significant, as I also wanted to take Desiree and the children.

Our Pastor said he wanted to take a group of people to visit the Revival and also to Milan in Tennessee where another Revival had broken out. Over 1,000 people from a population of 7,000 had committed their lives to Jesus in just a few months. The cost of the trip was £1,800, which we didn't have, as we were just about managing to pay our bills. I talked to Desiree about it and we prayed it through. *At the same time we told our Pastor that we wanted to go and believed the money was going to come from somewhere.*

Over the next month or so we continued to pray daily about it but there was no sign of the money. I must admit that Desiree had much stronger faith than I did about the trip and kept saying, "I know that the money is coming". Then one Sunday our Pastor's wife reminded us that we would need to pay for the trip by the following week. We were concerned; all we had managed to scrape together towards the cost was £150. We prayed and prayed that week, but still nothing came in. On the Tuesday I felt somewhat despondent and called to see John Marshall, a godly friend who had been mentoring me for a while. He and his wife Joan were wonderful to us as a family and they told us they were always there if we needed them for anything. (Nothing has changed and they are still exactly the same today.) I drove to their house and knocked on the door. When John opened it I blurted out, "John we need to pray together". I told him of the situation. We stood in his living room and asked the Lord to intervene and provide the money as we strongly believed that Lord wanted us to go and visit the Revivals.

I went from John's house to our midweek evening meeting at church, which was about a twelve-minute journey. As I entered the church one of our young people tapped me on the shoulder and handed me an envelope saying "I have been asked to let you have this, but the person who is giving it wants to remain anonymous. It was bulky and felt like it was burning a hole in my pocket during the prayer session. I opened it in my car after the meeting to find £200! I thanked God for His provision and said, "Right we still need £1,450". We continued to pray in earnest about it. The very next morning at work our Payroll Manager came to see me and said "Moray, I have some very good news for you. You'll be pleased to know that on Friday's pay run you will receive a £700 tax rebate".

I sat there and thanked God once again as I now had over £1,000. The next day Desiree's father turned up unannounced at our house and handed her a cheque for £750. He said it was a gift; he had just received the payment from the insurance company in settlement of the claim for his back injury. We had no idea that there was any money coming his way and had forgotten about the accident which had happened some years before. We also had another gift from someone in the church, which enabled us to give what was right to the Lord and we were left with exactly £1,800. *Wow! What an amazing God!*

The Revival in Pensacola was incredible and it was an experience that will stay with us for as long as we live. We queued outside the church in the hot sun to get into the meetings. Desiree was interviewed whilst in the queue by a radio station who had sent reporters along to see what was happening. I had never before witnessed so many people running to the altar as they did every night that we were there. God was present in the meetings; there was no doubt of that. After five days we went on to Milan in Tennessee and saw God was moving in a very powerful way there too. The Pastor of the church confessed to us that he was a pastor who didn't pray much, but was persuaded to visit the Pensacola Revival and God impacted his life in a very powerful way. He went back to his own church where Revival broke out immediately and spread to other fellowships in the area.

While we were there we witnessed some other events which were proof that God was pouring out His Spirit on the town. An evening with a Southern Gospel band had been arranged for our Pastor who was a fan of that genre of music. They drove up from Nashville in their tour bus and arrived a few hours before the meeting was due to start. They pulled up in the car park in a bus and turned off the engine. The very moment they did, the power of God fell in the bus. They had no idea that Revival had broken out in the church at all. They just thought that they had come to do another church gig. They were so powerfully hit by the presence of God that they all slumped onto the floor and were unable to get up for three hours. They tried to explain in the meeting what had happened, but when they tried to speak they just wept. They were a great bunch of guys who were all evidently impacted by what God had done.

Our daughter Bethan was six at the time and we had been trying for another baby for a while and were undergoing medical investigations to determine the reason. Desiree found the situation distressing, we prayed but nothing happened. After about four years of trying Desiree declared to God, "Lord, I am giving the situation to you. If you want me to have another baby, that's fine, if you don't want me to, then that's fine as well". We didn't tell anyone about the prayer. On the next Sunday morning a prophecy came through our Pastor for Desiree where the Lord said that He had closed her womb but He would open it again at an appointed time and she would have more children. We were amazed and believed God because we had not mentioned her prayer to anyone.

During the time at Milan, about a year later, Desiree was praying with a few women from the church when one, who had no knowledge of the situation, looked intently at Desiree and said to her. "The Lord has closed your womb because you still have bitterness towards your father about a situation that happened during your teens. You need to forgive him now". Desiree confessed that she was right and forgave her father in prayer right there and then. That very evening in our own church a prophecy was given that a woman would return from the USA expecting a baby. *To our surprise and joy Desiree became pregnant within the next two weeks!*

Nine months later our son was born; whom we named him after Samuel in the Old Testament. A woman called Hannah, who could not conceive, was observed by the Prophet Eli, who saw her as she prayed quietly. He actually thought she was drunk as he could only see her lips moving and that she appeared greatly distressed. She promised the Lord that if He gave her a son she would give him to the Lord's service. Eli spoke about her situation and said "Go in peace and may the Lord grant your request". Sometime later Hannah became pregnant and called her son Samuel. When we look at our son we know that he is a miracle from the

Lord. We also had another daughter two years later called Elena Grace. God is so good.

When we returned from America we became involved in a local Mission that was led by a very experienced Anglican Evangelist called Daniel Cousins. At one meeting I played in the music team. The worship was very traditional and different from what I was used to. It felt like hard work to play in that environment. Daniel gave a very short message that was excellent, a serious one but it was mingled with humour. He said that he was going to say a prayer, which was a prayer of Salvation to accept Jesus as Lord and Saviour. It was very like the one that Desiree prayed in our neighbour's kitchen years before. He explained that if anyone wanted to repeat the prayer, or say it silently in their heart that God would hear them. As he prayed I said to myself with a very negative attitude, "If anyone responds to that it will be a miracle". What happened next taught me a valuable lesson. At the end of the prayer he said "While every eye is closed and every head is bowed, I would ask that if you repeated that prayer of Salvation to raise your hand to signify to me that you want to receive Jesus as Lord". I sat there with my eyes closed expecting nothing to happen. As I did I heard Daniel say. "Thank you I see that hand. Thank you I see those two hands there. Thank you Sir you can put your hand down. Thank you Madam". He went on saying thank you a number of times. Some ladies were weeping in the church as they were touched by the Holy Spirit. I said sorry to the Lord and since then have tried never to judge what will happen when an altar call is given. God can change lives immediately. It is always the Holy Spirit that touches hearts and it was no different that evening.

Some years later we visited the Toronto Airport Vineyard Church, known worldwide for the "Toronto Blessing". My Pastor visited the church in the early days of the Holy Spirit outpouring. Amazing things had been happening. There had been some negative press about the events from reporters who perhaps didn't understand the powerful move of the Holy Spirit. I wanted to go there but didn't have the opportunity until twelve years after it started. Before visiting I spent the day with an elderly well-respected minister, David Morris, to ask his opinion as to whether we should pay the church a visit. He reassured me that it was not unusual and that we should definitely go.

We arrived at the church, which is an enormous, converted factory unit holding thousands. A Pastors' conference had finished the day before, which meant that when we entered the church there were only about one hundred people in the main sanctuary. There was a sea of empty chairs on both our right and our left. A worship team sang led by a lady with big curly hair. Another very similar-looking lady accompanied her, playing a recorder. A middle-aged man was very gently playing the drums. As I walked in I judged the attendees and the music which sounded like a school assembly and thought to myself, "This is going to be hard work". God knew differently. As soon as we got to our seats I was overcome with emotion and wept, continuing all through the worship. Desiree can verify the fact that I hardly ever cry. That evening I had a powerful life-changing encounter with the Lord, which I am very grateful for.

We attended the evening session the next day. This time the building was packed with people. Instead of many empty chairs we struggled to find a place to sit. On this occasion the worship was conducted by a keyboard player who sang, accompanied by two women. I must be honest and say that the style of music was not to my taste, but as soon as I got to my seat I started to weep again and did so for the whole of the worship time, which lasted about an hour. The meeting was a Healing Service and we saw God move powerfully during the evening, touching and healing people who were sick and disabled. I knew that the Lord was calling me to preach and I thought how wonderful it would be to be used by God in that way.

God had started speaking to my heart about what He wanted me to do for Him and something similar was happening to Desiree also. *We knew the Lord was going to reveal His Plan for us and we prayed for this. We both had a strong desire to serve Him in whichever way He would lead us.*

Speaking in Latvia for the Business Men's Fellowship

I love this picture with my wonderful wife Desiree
in July 2008 at Althorpe House where Princess
Diana grew up

Being interviewed on Radio in Latvia

I say to people, don't tell me that God doesn't have a sense of humour, because I now do the very thing that I once despised. Street preaching in the town of Caerphilly

Me with my mother who is now in her eighties and
my six fantastic kids

Not bad for an overweight 50 year old. On holiday in France
having fun with my then 14 year old daughter Bethan

Chapter 16

Hearing and Missing and Ignoring the Word of The Lord

Having read this far you will know just some of the many, many times when God has moved in our lives. There have been occasions when I have heard the Lord speak and obeyed the instruction as well as times when I have missed what He was saying. Regretfully I have to admit I have even ignored Him on occasions, thinking I knew better, or simply because I still wanted to do things my way. I often joke about the title for my second book. It would be entitled 'How to miss the voice of God – My Life'. When I have gone my own way, it has been a painful experience in one way or another.

Desiree and I had only been Christians for a few months when a team of Prophets visited our church. Four of them were from America and one from London. None of them knew our situation, or us. The Lord spoke to us very clearly through them; we were greatly blessed. An American lady prophesied to us giving very clear instructions to study the word of God on the subject of handling money. Some months later, at my desk with my Bible closed asked God to show me what to read first. As I said "Amen" and reached out for my Bible, a voice as clear as my own said "Read Acts Chapter Five". Startled, I asked myself "did I imagine hearing that?" I had read the book of Acts a couple of times before but honestly had no recollection of reading anything about money in this chapter. I found it contained the story of Ananias and Sapphira. During the early days of the church

Christians shared their belongings. They often sold their possessions and property, and gave the income to the Apostles who in turn used it to help out those in need. This couple decided to sell a field and give the money to the Apostles. They kept back some of the proceeds of the sale but pretended they were giving the full amount they had received for the land. The Apostle Peter had divine revelation of this situation and told Ananias that he had lied both to men and to God. When Ananias heard his words he fell down dead and the same fate befell his wife three hours later when she lied too. Great fear spread throughout the church as a result of this. I took the message to heart; there is nothing we can hide from God. He knows our thoughts and the motives of our hearts. There have many times I have read scripture and it has applied to my circumstances. At times it has made me aware of something I should do, on other occasions when I have been going through a trial, I have found encouraging words in the pages of my Bible, which gave me hope about specific situations. *God really does move in varied and wonderful ways.*

A team of people from Milan, Tennessee came to visit our church for a few days. I played bass guitar with a few of them in the worship team and four of them stayed at our home. We enjoyed their company and became very close. Matt Pratt, who is still one of my closest friends, and Rick Waycaster who later became the Pastor of their church. At that time they needed a bass player in their worship team and invited us to move to America saying, "You can join our band". A friend of theirs on the team, a wealthy businessman would give me a job. When we realised they sincerely meant this, Desiree and I prayed about it every day asking the Lord to confirm it in some way so we would know it to be God's Will. The idea of living and working in America had always appealed to me and I reasoned this might well be the Lord speaking to me. Matt and his wife Renee came to stay with us for a holiday a few months later and told us that their church were considering opening a Christian radio station in the Arkansas area. If the idea worked, the church would offer me the Sales Manager's position, which would involve generating revenue through advertising for the station. The job would be well paid and we would be able to work at in the church too, a wonderful opportunity as we love helping others in practical ways.

We both continued to pray fervently about it and arranged to visit the area. When we arrived in Magnolia, Arkansas after a long drive from Milan, Matt took me to the church, as he had some odd jobs to finish. I remember very clearly standing in the main sanctuary on my own while Matt was busy in his office, asking the Lord. "Father, is this where you want me to be?" I didn't hear an audible voice but I knew in my heart that He didn't want me there. The trouble was though that I wanted to be there, to start a new life in America with Desiree and the children. These people wanted us to move there and join their church. For the next year, my prayers focussed moving there. We prayed persistently and wanted the answer from God, "Go to America", but we didn't hear the Lord telling us to go.

I contacted the American sales company that had offered me work, asking if they had any suitable positions for me in the USA. The European Director, who had been headhunting me, consulted his best friend, the manager of the Mississippi and Tennessee Region. He offered me a job; the Director even said he would help me with a visa. We were able to afford another visit by this time. While we were there we looked at property; we were offered gifts of furniture and even a car! I persuaded myself that it must be God's plan for us and my excitement started to build up.

A period of about eighteen months had passed since Matt and Rick had first suggested that we could emigrate. During that time I didn't mention anything about it to my pastor. I believed that if everything was in place before I told him our plans, he would have to agree that it was God who had made all of this happen. Many times over the years God has shown us that He doesn't think the way we do. His ways are higher than our ways. My experience is that He handles things in a very different manner to that which one might expect.

On our visit we stayed in Milan for two weeks and had a great time. The pastor of a church that many of our friends attended was taken ill and hospitalised. The congregation thought he was going to die, as he was very sick. The members prayed constantly throughout the week. For the next Sunday meeting a replacement speaker from Chicago, a prophet, was invited to minister. He had prophesied on radio that the Lord was going to send a Revival to Pensacola two years before it actually happened.

That afternoon he flew from Chicago to Memphis, then drove to the church. He preached and then prophesied to people throughout the evening continuing into the night. At 1am he was praying for a small line of people in the main sanctuary. The church was almost empty by that time. Eventually he came to me and asked, "What do you want?" I replied "Direction". I was hoping that the Lord would clearly say that I was to move with my family to America; but he didn't say anything about that at all but repeated several times about something which remains a calling on my life. The Lord said that I would be used to minister to broken people and that I should preach His gospel. I felt a great certainty as God spoke through this man and knew in my heart that it was true. I had always felt a burning desire to preach and lead the Lost to the Lord. This feeling had become much stronger. I was thrilled about this call to preach but wondered why God hadn't said anything about us moving over to the States.

The prophet's had such an effect that night that another meeting was arranged for the following Friday evening. The church was packed with over five hundred people in attendance. The meeting was similar to the previous one, there were many prophecies, healings and outpourings of the Holy Spirit. The whole group at the front of the church wanted to receive a word from the Lord. The prophet came near to us and then moved away in another direction. The meeting was still going on at 2 am. Desiree is a very talented hair stylist and beautician, and was painting a lady's toe nails with a funky pattern in the reception when the prophet's wife walked over and said "Hey, that's neat". They got talking and Desiree said "We are going home to Wales tomorrow and we haven't had a word from the Lord". She took Desiree by the hand; came to find me and led us over to the prophet who by this time was looking exhausted.

The lady said to her husband "Please pray for these guys as they are going home to Wales tomorrow morning". He looked at me but didn't seem to recognise me from the previous meeting. He asked me again, "What do you want?" I answered as before "Direction". Inside, however I was asking the Lord to show me if He wanted me to work and live in America. The prophet laid hands on us both and started to pray. After a minute or so he started to prophesy and said staring at me and pointing to the floor, "The Lord says to you, this is not where I want you to be". He continued in that vein for a while and prophesied to Desiree about numerous things that were specifically for her. Gazing at me intently he said, "You will preach my Gospel". As soon as he said it I was in great travail and I was bent double with the pain. Each time I straightened up he said "And the Lord says you will preach my Gospel" The same thing happened each time, five times altogether; each time he spoke I felt yet more pain. The prophecy went on for some time and he finished saying, "The Lord says that in October or November He is going to tell you what He wants you to do for the next seven years".

There had been many prophecies regarding dates and so on through both of the meetings so we just accepted it. We went home saddened that it was not the Lord's will for us to move to USA. At the same time, though I felt very eager about this call to do the one thing I had always wanted - to preach the word of God. We determined to pray for what the Lord was going to say next.

Once again I didn't tell anyone about the prophecy, but instead prayed about it all through October and November, asking the Lord what He wanted us to do for the seven-year period. I got no answer and by the last Sunday in November I was feeling quite despondent and even thought that maybe the prophet had got it wrong. The desire to preach was still growing steadily but I had not heard anything about the seven-year period. At the end of our evening meeting Pastor invited anyone who wanted prayer to come forward. People went up to be prayed for and I was the last in line. I didn't have a very good attitude at that moment, but went up anyway. Pastor prayed for various people and eventually came to me. I was amazed at what he said. He laid hands on me and looked me saying, "Seven years. Seven years. Seven years". He continued to pray, then afterwards he spoke to the church explaining what the seven years meant. In Israel in Old Testament times, slaves would serve their masters for a period of time leading up to when they could be freed to go their own way if they wished. Some would nail their ear to the door post of their master's house signifying that they would like to stay and not be set free. I believed that the Lord was speaking to me through my Pastor, so I went to see him the following week and explained what had happened. I felt that it was right to remain with my Pastor for that period of time, which we did and much more. He has since moved to the USA himself. During those years I had increasing opportunities to preach. Over time we moved to a new fellowship and are now actively involved in all aspects of evangelism. It is very exciting.

God has been good. In ministry I have had the privilege of seeing many people make decisions for Christ when I have either shared my own life story or preached the Gospel; but the Lord hasn't stopped there! We have seen God perform many miraculous healings. There are too many to mention, but they range from bones snapping back into place, relief from insomnia, joints repaired, neuralgia cured, swellings reducing instantly, open wounds closing, throat conditions clearing up instantly, headaches disappearing, bales palsy disappearing, and many other wonderful examples of health being restored as people are prayed for.

Some years ago I was asked to visit the city of Riga, in Latvia, to share my story with some Christian business groups as well as holding a one day sales psychology course at a college. Walking into the airport my mobile phone rang. I answered to hear the voice of Steve Hyde, who is the pastor of a thriving church in the Midlands. He knew that I would be travelling to Riga at some time but didn't know when.

He asked "Moray - where are you?" I answered "I am walking into Bristol airport, on my way to speak in Latvia." Steve replied, "Well that makes sense because the Lord impressed on me to call you. He wants you to know that after you share your testimony and people accept Jesus, you are to invite the sick to be prayed for, because the Lord will be present to heal!"

I thanked Steve for his obedience in making the call and boarded the plane with great anticipation. I had prayed for the sick but not seen anything happen. I said to the Lord, "Father, if that was you, I receive it." On that trip I saw many lives changed as people received Jesus, through hearing my story. I don't know the language, so had to speak through an interpreter.

The first event was held in a large wooden cabin which was actually a men's sauna and appeared to be in the middle of nowhere. The ground was covered in snow and the cabin stood next to a large lake that was completely frozen over. I had a lovely meal and spoke in front of a large open fire.

As instructed, afterwards I invited anyone who needed a healing touch from Jesus to come forward. The first person I prayed for was a young man in his twenties. The interpreter asked the man what he wanted. The young man explained he had been in a bad car accident some years before and had damaged his knee, causing great pain and limiting movement. I knelt down and placed my right hand on his kneecap and started to pray asking the Lord to repair any damage in the knee.

As I prayed I felt intense heat come into my hand. So much so, that it felt as if my hand was red hot. I exclaimed to my interpreter "My hand feels as if it is one fire and this guy's knee is very hot as well. Ask him if he can feel anything." He didn't get a chance to ask however, because unknown to us the young man could speak good English. He exclaimed loudly, "I can feel, I can feel it!"

After praying the young man moved his knee bending it, kicking out his leg and explained that all the pain and discomfort had completely disappeared. I met the interpreter again some years later and he is still in contact with the young man. He explained the pain has never returned and he now works in the UK.

The next person I prayed for was a wealthy businessman. He had driven me to the lodge in his car. He didn't speak any English at all. Through the interpreter I learned that the man had been experiencing very bad back pain for some years. I prayed in the same way as before. I felt no heat as I did the first time, so wondered if anything had happened.

The next day I spoke at another location. As people arrived the businessman came through the door with a huge smile on his face. He caught my eye and pointed to his back, put his thumbs up and nodded. It was obvious that something remarkable had happened.

I spoke with him through the interpreter. What he told me was incredible. I give God all of the glory! This is what he said. "I am the owner of a private hospital and clinic in Riga where I employ a number of Doctors. I have had severe back pain for many years. As a result I have only been able to sleep for no more than two hours at a time. My Doctors have tried everything to relieve the pain but nothing has worked. Last night after you prayed I went home and slept all night for the first time in years. My pain has completely disappeared!"

I also learned from the interpreter that the pain had not returned for this man either. God is faithful and honours His word.

On one occasion I was asked to pray for a person who was in a coma and close to death. The person in question had been very ill for some time. The request was for the sick person to regain lucidity to allow a relative to talk to them about Jesus. I prayed with another Christian at a prayer meeting in our church. We called on the name of the Lord at 8 pm asking Him to intervene and give the relative a chance to speak to the person before they died. We were delighted to learn that the person regained consciousness while the relative was at the bedside in hospital at exactly 8 pm. God is just amazing!

Very often the Holy Spirit will give me a Word of Knowledge about situations, where I will mention specific conditions. People put their hands up saying "That's me!" All the Glory goes to God, because people are healed in the name of Jesus. I have no power to heal at all. It is Jesus who heals them.

Once, when I was preaching at a baptism, I gave a Word of Knowledge regarding a painful twisted back. At the end of the meeting a lady came to see me and said that she had the condition which had been causing her great discomfort. A new Christian in our church named Lee, who has become a great friend, was standing nearby and I remembered him saying that he would really love to witness a healing when I prayed in the name of Jesus.

Calling him over, I explained that the lady had responded to the word I gave about the condition. I said "Let's pray!" - and with the lady's permission, I placed Lee's hand on her back with my hand next to his. I started to pray asking Jesus to heal the lady. After a few seconds she jerked and twisted in a way that I could only describe as like a turnstile in the entrance to a football ground. As she did this there was a loud clunking sound. In fact she moved so violently that the force of it pushed us both backwards to a distance of about two or three feet.

Lee said, "Wow" quite loudly as it happened. I asked the lady, "Goodness me, did you feel that happen?" She replied "Feel what happen?" I explained what had just taken place. She looked somewhat surprised at this. I asked her to move her back in a way that would normally be painful. She did so twisting, bending over and stretching and looked at me with a big smile on her face exclaiming that the pain had completely gone!

I have many other stories that I could share like this, but there are just too many to mention. I never tire of seeing the Lord move in this way.

Having experienced the high life in the past, I sometimes missed the buzz of how stimulating and enthralling it was. The opportunity came some years ago to get involved once again in a Financial Services business with some former colleagues. It was going to start in a small way, building a local business to serve the community; but before I knew it we were talking about building a pan European company with offices all over the UK. We devised product ranges and a strategy to take the business nation-wide. The thought of building it up from scratch thrilled me. I prayed about it and realised that it would mean changing my original plan. Desiree didn't support the decision I had made because she was concerned what could happen if it went wrong and didn't want to go through that dreadful pain again.

I enjoyed the planning, the risk and the pioneering element. I trained new advisers to generate significant levels of business and some of them have gone on to greater things as a result of it. *It was a thrill for me, but the truth was that all the time I knew that it was not really the will of God for me.* For a while, I simply yearned prove to myself and other people that I could do it all over again. The success addiction had tempted me. I was now much less focused on my spiritual walk, instead concentrating on finance, my business and career. I had a call on my life but lost my way temporarily.

Some Christians would say that the Devil had set a trap for me to fall into. I don't know whether that is true. If it was indeed a trap, I didn't just fall into it. Rather, plunged into it with the passion of an Olympic high diver. I lost a considerable amount of money and for a long period of time, we struggled financially. The bad events resurfaced, tormenting me. The battles with stress and depression inevitably returned. It was my fault entirely causing a very painful time for Desiree and I, and all because I made a decision according to my own desires, completely ignoring what I knew the Lord was saying to me.

I am absolutely certain that if I had done things *His* way it would have gone well. I went astray and followed what *I* thought was right and ended up paying the price for my foolishness. The Bible speaks of the old 'You' which is what each person is before coming to Christ. When you accept Jesus as Lord you learn to 'Die to self'. This means that the old person no longer steers the direction of your life, as you are a new creation in Christ.

When I got involved in Financial Services again, I had allowed the 'Old Man' in me to get up and take control taking me in entirely the wrong direction.

Preaching at a church in Kirov, Russia on a recent trip

Praying for the sick in Kirov

People receiving Jesus in Kirov

Demonstrating a key point in Kirov

I have spoken in many places, but never a in a sauna until I visited Riga in Latvia

Inviting people to hear my story at a sales psychology seminar

Chapter 17

Getting to the point

The greatest moments of my Christian life have been when people have come to know Jesus, after hearing the gospel or through me sharing my testimony. I have always told people about my faith and I am not ashamed of the Gospel of Jesus Christ. It has changed my own life and I am deeply grateful for His sacrifice on the Cross. I will continue to talk about Him till the end of my days.

I have knocked doors, preached on the street, spoken in schools, tents and many other places. Sometimes when I have been singing in a group or playing a guitar in a team outside in a town, both Desiree and I have then stood up and declared what Jesus has done in our lives. Often I was blessed to have a microphone. God must surely have a sense of humour because the very thing that I despised about Christians I am now doing! Even more incredible is that I am training other people to do so. Sometimes it is referred to as "cringe factor evangelism". This doesn't bother me in the least; if by hearing our witness people come to Christ, then that is all that matters. It used to make me cringe too, before I knew the truth, that Jesus died for me; but I have seen all kinds of amazing things happen as we have shared the Gospel on the streets.

If I see people evangelising in that way I will go over and encourage them because it can be a difficult thing to do. You never know what might happen when you speak the word of God. It is a living word and **"it will not return to Him**

void". Over the centuries many people have come to Christ through this type of preaching. Due to the politically correct world in which we now live I do not know how much longer that it will be permitted to continue, but I have a desire to do it.

I love sharing the good news about Jesus on a one to one basis; in fact our ministry is named "Gospel One To One. I have had countless such conversations; here are three instances where telling others of my experiences, the Holy Spirit has spoken into their heart and they realised that Jesus is the answer to their own situation. On occasions I can be rather confrontational in my style and embrace the challenge when given an opportunity to talk about Jesus.

The Atheist

During my life I have only ever met one or two people who were true atheists. Many people say they are atheists, but are in fact agnostics. In other words, they are not really sure what they believe and sometimes they avoid talking about matters such as life after death because of fear. An atheist can be described as a person who reads the Bible, books on evolution, Darwinism and other theories. After doing so they make a deliberate decision not to believe God's Word and adapt their beliefs from various other sources.

Some people may have read 'Chariots of the Gods' or similar books but have not taken the time to read the whole Bible. In my opinion someone can only be considered an atheist after thoroughly reading and studying the Bible, theories in opposition to it and then deciding on which to believe.

In our first couple of years as Christians my wife's parents had some married friends that they regularly met up with. The wife was a follower of Christ, whereas the husband was an atheist having studied the Bible and opposing literature. He had read the Bible from cover to cover several times. He also had a great interest in Science and was well read on Evolution and similar theories. Although our beliefs differed greatly we got on well.

In the course of our conversations I learned that he had experienced a difficult childhood. His twin brother died tragically in a house fire, which he had escaped from. His mother eventually left home, as she was unable to cope. This had made him very hardhearted and he would attempt to disprove the Gospel at any opportunity. We met a number of times over a year or so. We always had deep discussions and debates. Sometimes the debates became heated with us both raising our voices. We had a verbal tennis match. He said, "There is no evidence that God exists". I replied, "Just look at Creation" and gave lots of examples of how the world had to have been designed. I said, "Take for instance the human lung, I have read that if you were to lay one out with all its parts and sections, it would fill a tennis court". He agreed that was correct but then expounded on the Big Bang theory or something similar. He said, "God doesn't exist". I responded *"The fool says in his heart there is no God"*. These types of heated exchanges usually lasted for an hour or two. It is quite amusing when I think back about it because both of us actually used to look forward to meeting so that we could have these verbal duels.

One day we were in my mother-in-law's kitchen having another very heated discussion, when he said confidently,

"Do you know that there is only one chromosome less in a monkey than there is in a man"? I answered "Yes I do". He carried on "So that must prove that apes evolved into human beings". I thought about what he had said for a few seconds and replied "I will tell you why there is only just one less chromosome in a monkey. It is because God made it that way". He stared at me and said nothing for a few moments and we then carried on talking. A few weeks later I heard that he had started attending church with his wife and had become a Christian. I rejoiced in the wonderful news, but had no idea what had caused his change of heart. We lost contact with him for a while, until one day when he turned up on our doorstep with a colleague from his church. He was involved in an Evangelistic Team working in the Welsh valleys and was sold out for God. "Fantastic!" I thought.

We sat in my lounge and I asked him, "Tell me, what happened to make you want to go to church and accept Christ"? He replied, "Do you remember the time when we were in your mother-in-law's kitchen and I talked to you about the chromosome difference between a man and a monkey?" "Yes" I replied. He continued, "Well, what you said about God designing a monkey like that made me reconsider. So that evening at home I got out my Bible and started to read. Within a short time I realised that the Bible was the Truth and I gave my life to Christ."

Over the years I have seen God touch the hardest of hearts. People who I had believed would probably never accept Christ. His is able to speak to highly intellectual people by revealing the truth of the Gospel. In fact He can speak to anyone. It is an incredible miracle that I never tire of seeing.

The Traditional Church-Goer

I have been very blessed over the years to lead a number of work colleagues to Jesus. I am certain that anyone who has ever worked with me would confirm that I never hid the fact that I am a follower of Christ. I tried to bring Jesus into my conversations during the working day in one way or another.

When I sold my Financial Services business I was retained as the branch manager of the office in Swansea. We were on a recruitment drive and I contacted an applicant called Peter. We had a chat on the phone and I invited him into my office for an informal interview. He was in his late forties and had recently moved back to Wales after a very successful career in the City as a Marketing Director for a very large pharmaceutical company. He came across very well during our meeting when we got onto the subject of Tenby where he lived. He told me that he owned a small guesthouse there which his wife managed.

He said, "Have a look at our web site when you are online". I put his address in my search engine and within a few moments I was looking at his web pages. The site had a bold heading, which read "Christian Run, Family Guesthouse". I said "Hey, that's fantastic I am a Christian as well, how long have you been following the Lord?". He said, "I go to church with my wife in Tenby. I'm a Methodist". "That's terrific" I replied, "When did you decide to follow Jesus?" He replied "Follow Him?" I said, "You know what I mean, I made a decision some years ago to follow Jesus and became a Born Again Christian and have never looked back". He looked at me a little awkwardly and said, "Oh no, I don't think that I'm Born Again". I replied, "Well, if you don't think you are then you are probably right, you are not".

We met on two more occasions and he joined the company. He was an extremely professional adviser. Over the months I worked with him I brought God into conversations and we had some in-depth discussions. He believed that you didn't need to be born again to go to Heaven. I asked him as I have done with many people, "Tell me Peter, do you believe that Jesus Christ is exactly who He said He is?" "Yes of course" he replied. I then asked, "Well, do you believe that the Bible is true?" "Yes of course I do" he replied. I continued "Do you think that Jesus would ever tell a lie then?" "Definitely not" was his answer. I then quoted John 3:5 "***I tell you the truth, no one can see the kingdom of God unless he is born again.***" "What do you think of that scripture then?" I asked. His answer like many others was "Oh I don't believe that is true". I replied "Well you just said that Jesus wouldn't say something that was a lie". I could see that he was irritated so I stopped there.

The discussions continued over a period of months. Sometimes we talked for an hour or two in the evening when the other staff had gone home. We agreed on many points except fundamental scriptures like this.

One day after yet another heated dialogue I said "Peter, I have got to say that based on all of our conversations I believe you are so close to the truth. Peter you are almost a Christian". He was visibly annoyed by this, so we left the matter there, knowing that what I had said was confrontational. Sometimes the truth must simply be declared. I love to read about the famous Evangelist Smith

Wigglesworth; he once said that when you preach the gospel you would either make the listener mad or glad. On that day Peter was definitely mad with me. I left the office in a hurry that day for an appointment and forgot all about what had happened between us.

The next week he came to sit at my desk with a very serious look on his face. He explained that when he had gone home after that conversation, he decided to go on the Internet, trying to find information on the Methodist Church web site about being a Born Again Christian. He eventually came to a site that contained a number of sermons by John Wesley, the famous Methodist preacher. When he preached the Gospel many people would turn their lives over to Christ there and then. Peter said, "I found this sermon by John Wesley called 'Almost a Christian'. I read it and it has really disturbed me. Can we meet to discuss it?", "No problem" I replied enthusiastically. We met a few days later in the early evening when everyone had left the office. I visited the Wesley web site and printed off the sermon and read it thoroughly. The message was preached in the year 1741 and was very clear. It explained that going to church, being a good person, singing in the choir, giving money and even praying didn't matter at all. None of that would get you to Heaven, unless you gave your life to Jesus Christ. It is a wonderful sermon, which I recommend.

I had explained to Peter on a number of occasions what the sermon contained. Predominately, the vital importance of making a decision to follow Jesus, to make Him Lord of your life, to repent of all of your sin and to turn from our own self-will to God's way. I had explained when someone does that and means it from their heart then a miracle happens and they become Born Again by the Spirit of God. The Holy Spirit literally dwells inside them and their lives are never the same. The only way into Heaven is just as Jesus says: -

"I am the way the truth and the life. No one comes to the Father except through Me". (John 14:6 NIV)

I looked forward to the meeting with Peter and prayed to the Lord to give me guidance. We discussed the Wesley message at great length and I even shared part of my own journey to faith in Christ. But I still couldn't get Peter, a well-educated and intelligent man, to understand what the message truly meant. As a result we kept getting stuck on the same point, arguing in circles. I went over it again and again but he just didn't understand. I prayed silently "Lord please guide me". I looked at my watch and realised that we had been talking for two hours. I asked him "Can I explain simply to you why Jesus died on the Cross?" He agreed and I went to the corner of the office and brought over a stand up flipchart. I said "Let me show you something that was in a little tract that was given to me, that both challenged and annoyed me years ago". "Sure" he replied.

I spent the next five minutes talking about the tract that Mike had given me and did my best to draw the simple diagram on the pad that explained the Fall of Man and the reason that Jesus paid the penalty for our sin. I was concentrating on what I was saying and drawing and so didn't notice what was happening with Peter. After a little while I looked at him to see that his eyes were full of tears. I asked "Peter, do you believe that is true"? "I do," he said.

continued, "Would you like to say a prayer with me and ask Jesus to come into your heart?" Yes please" he replied.

We sat in the office and I led him through a simple prayer where He asked Jesus to forgive him of his sins, and made Him Lord of his life. I suppose the way that I got through to Peter was by communicating the message in a way that he could relate to. He had been in many meetings over the years where a flipchart had been used. My drawings as shown later were not exceptional but the Holy Spirit used those simple drawings to open Peter's heart. Peter was transformed and is now bold in proclaiming his faith in Jesus Christ and is even a volunteer for the Bible Society. *Praise God!*

The Worldly Church-Goer

Another recruit called James joined the office from a banking background. He was a very pleasant chap and was very popular with the team in the office. He was extremely intelligent and had won a difficult quiz game on television. I let him know that I was a Christian on his first day in the job. He told me "I am a Christian and I go to our local church every Sunday". "That's great" I thought. As he got more familiar with colleagues I noticed that he swore a lot and even took the name of the Lord in vain. This disturbed me because if a person has truly given their life to Jesus the last thing they would do is use the name of Jesus Christ as a swear word. I decided when the time was right that I would challenge Him.

It wasn't very long and an opportunity arose, when we were alone. I said "James can I ask you a personal question?" "Yes of course" he replied. I said "To be totally honest with you, I am a little confused. You say you are a Christian, yet you use profane language and have even taken the name of the Lord in vain". He looked embarrassed and said that he didn't realise he had done so. I said "Imagine a drunk on the street was being spoken to by a person who was trying to help him from a local church. During the conversation the so-called Christian used profane language. I think you'd agree that even a drunk person would realise that something was wrong". James agreed and the language he used quickly changed.

I couldn't leave it there though, so I spoke to him on a number of occasions and asked him when he had made a decision to follow Jesus. He admitted that he had never done that, but that he did believe the Bible. I asked him as I had Peter - whether he thought that Jesus was in fact who He said He was and what he thought of the same verse of scripture. *"I tell you the truth, no one can see the kingdom of God unless he is born again".* His answer was just the same as Peter's.

We had many conversations and as with Peter we had a great deal in common. However, once again, we got stuck on that same fundamental truth. One Friday evening we were alone in the office and soon got onto the subject of the Lord. We talked about Heaven and discussed that no matter how good someone is, whether they go to church or give to charity they will not be able to enter Heaven unless their name is written in the Book of Life. The only way of getting there is to be a true follower of Jesus. We spoke of how no one would be able to enter the kingdom of God through his or her own righteousness or indeed by doing good works: -

"All our righteous acts are like filthy rags". (Isaiah 64: 6 NIV)

I used another verse to explain that a commitment is required from the heart: -

"Not everyone who says to me, 'Lord, Lord,' will enter the kingdom of heaven, but only he who does the will of my Father who is in heaven. Many will say to me on that day, 'Lord, Lord, did we not prophesy in your name, and in your name drive out demons and perform many miracles?' Then I will tell them plainly, 'I never knew you. Away from me, you evildoers!' (Matthew 7: 21-23 NIV)

As we spoke I noticed from his expression that he had had a sudden realisation - there was nothing he could do to earn his way into Heaven. He realised that he was a lost sheep just like I had been. Jesus had saved me by His Grace. I asked him "Do you want to leave here tonight with complete assurance that if you died today you would be in Heaven with Jesus?" He looked at me and said "Moray I'm not ready yet". I replied "We will never be ready because there is nothing we can do of ourselves. Today is the day of Salvation. Don't put it off, we can deal with this now if you truly believe". "Yes I do believe" he replied. That was all I needed to hear. At that moment it felt that God's presence was very powerful in the office. I could clearly see that James was affected by it because he gasped sharply and held his breath for few a moments. His eyes filled with tears. I asked, "Would you like to receive Jesus as your Saviour now?" He answered "Yes, I would". We went through the prayer in the same way as I had with Peter. *God is truly amazing! I couldn't wait to tell Desiree the good news.*

Some time after that both Peter and James even assisted me in running a 'Look and See Christian Course' in the office with a number of other advisers. The three of us were witnessing of God's goodness. It was an encouraging period. Once Peter joined me when I spoke to a group of Christian businessmen and he shared his story of coming to Christ. *God is so good!*

My badly drawn diagrams

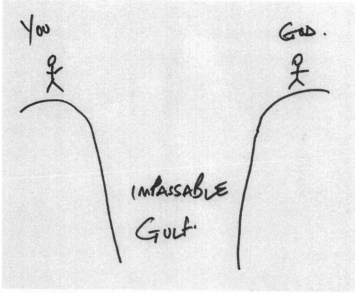

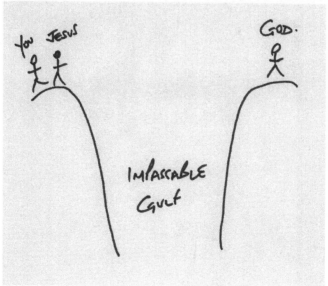

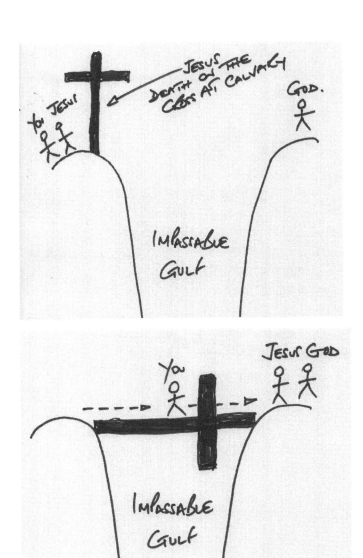

Chapter 18

What is Happening Now?
And What About You?

This is my story to date. My wife Desiree and I now serve in ministry as Evangelists and church leadership. After waiting a very long time, we are now fully involved in this. Once we knew in our hearts that it was God's will we began the work. It involves preaching, testifying, teaching and equipping the saints for the work of evangelising effectively. I love teaching (I teach adults for a living) and training as much as I did when I was in Sales. It is rewarding to see people's confidence grow through the training we provide.

I am also involved in The Full Gospel Business Men's Fellowship, which spreads the Gospel of Jesus Christ through an association for businessmen. It is a fantastic group, of men who have a desire and passion to share the good news of Jesus Christ.

Many people have helped, supported and encouraged us over the years and have become close friends; they are people who believed in us, inspired us, advised us and stuck with us even in our darkest hours. We are ever grateful to God for their input into our lives. Their help, prayers and advice cannot be measured.

My heart is to reach people with the message of the Gospel of Jesus Christ. It is the call of God on my life that I feel compelled to answer. God has always been faithful to me, so the very least I can do is to give my energy and drive to

Him by serving Him in the ministry that He has called me to. There is no greater joy than when I witness others accepting Jesus as their Saviour and Lord or bodies being healed of all kinds of sicknesses and diseases. Jesus Christ is still very much in the business of transforming lives, and He can transform yours. One of the really exciting parts is that I have been able to visit international countries to preach the Gospel and share my story. It is really very humbling.

Another exciting development has been teaching people sales psychology, which has proved to be a door for the Gospel message. I have held a few sales conferences in Russia and Latvia which were packed out with attendees. In Latvia, I shared my story in part throughout the day of the course. At the conference a man filmed all of the sessions. Before he left the college in the evening he accepted Jesus as Lord. I also invited people to an evening meal. A number of them came along, heard my testimony in full and received Jesus too!

In Perm in Russia I spoke at a smaller businessmen's dinner in a restaurant in the centre of the city. After the meal and sharing my story a number of people came to Christ. I also prayed for the sick during the evening.

As I was getting ready to leave the organiser of the event asked me if I could stay a little longer to speak about sales psychology, as there were a number of people who would be interested in hearing what I had to say. I had time to spare, so I spoke about communication.

This element of my courses has a lot of interaction and humour in it. Very soon, even though I was speaking through an interpreter, people were laughing and really getting involved in my practical demonstrations. I finished off by saying that using this method would lead to greater success in their businesses. Then I explained that although this is good, there is something much more important.; that every person needs to get right with God by asking Him for forgiveness for the things they have done wrong and making Him Lord of their lives. Doing this guarantees a future in eternity with Him. I gave another invitation and more people received Jesus.

Next I travelled on an overnight train to the city of Kirov where I held a sales conference with another packed audience, once again inviting people to a dinner I was speaking at that evening. People came along from the conference and at the dinner they received Jesus as Lord.

One thing that pleased me about my time in Kirov was that before the meal a number of the event organisers (went onto the street and invited people to join them in the restaurant for dinner so that they could hear my story. That evening a young lady who was invited tearfully got right with God. I prayed for her and mentioned I was preaching at the New Life church the next day, at both the morning and evening meetings. The day was fantastic and many people acknowledged Jesus as Lord. In the evening I was praying for people who made decisions for Jesus and came upon an older lady who was holding the hand of the girl at the restaurant.

She told me that after the meal she went home and explained to her mother what had happened. She invited her to the evening meeting the next day, where she gave her heart to the Lord. God is amazing!

Now, a personal question to you, the reader: "What about you?" You have read my story. Maybe you are going through a difficult time in your life and are searching for answers in a similar way that I was. Your issue could be financial like mine was, or to do with relationships, health, employment, family or something else. Whatever it is, there is no problem that is too big for Jesus. I have seen how God intervenes in the most difficult of circumstances, when people have lost all hope. Everything can change when God steps in. There is always an answer and that answer is Jesus.

Some years ago I was the after dinner speaker at a Businessmen's Fellowship meeting in Bridgend, South Wales. After sharing my testimony a number of people made decisions for Christ which as always, thrilled me. After the meeting a number of people came to speak to me. The last person I had a conversation with was a lady in her late fifties. She had been drinking a lot of alcohol during the evening. She told me that her husband had left her some years before, which devastated her, as it was sudden and totally unexpected. She explained that she had never got over it and that she could not forgive him. Now, many years on, she still cried every day about the situation. She was full of regret very bitter towards her ex husband. At one point she got loud and animated as I listened to her story. She asked me "Please tell me what I can do to make this hurt go away". I answered "Jesus can take all of this hurt away from you, but first of all you need to repent of your own sins and believe on the Lord Jesus Christ as Saviour and Lord. If you do that He will take away your hurt and your pain". When I had spoken she got angry and started to swear. I managed to calm her down eventually and she went on her way. Jesus is the only answer to removing bitterness, guilt, hurt and un-forgiveness. He brings peace love and joy to our lives.

Our problems can be very complex and originate in the past just as they did with this lady. Jesus can solve the problem and wash away years of pain. You just need to ask Him to be Lord of your life and cast all of your cares upon him.

"Come to me, all you who are weary and burdened, and I will give you rest. Take my yoke upon you and learn from me, for I am gentle and humble in heart, and you will find rest for your souls. For my yoke is easy and my burden is light." (Matthew 11: 28-30

I have spoken about confessing your sins and asking the Lord to forgive you in my story. You may be a really good person who attends a church on a regular basis. You may be someone who does many charitable works that are recognised by other people. You may be kind to your family and to others. But all this is of no consequence unless you have accepted Jesus Christ as your Saviour and Lord. God is holy and just and our sins demand that a penalty is paid. Jesus paid the penalty for the sins of everyone by His sacrifice on the Cross. If we accept Jesus as Saviour we can have a relationship with God and life everlasting.

There is absolutely nothing we can do to earn our way into Heaven. We have all sinned and need to repent of it which means turning away from it. If we judge ourselves by God's standards, the Ten Commandments, then we are all guilty.

Jesus said if we break just one of the commandments we are guilty of breaking them all. We have all lied, got angry, coveted, had sinful thoughts, have broken each one of the commandments at some point in our lives: -

"For all have sinned and fall short of the glory of God."
(Romans 3: 23 **NIV***)*

A long time ago the word sin was involved in archery. A circular target would be drawn on a wall and a number of arrows would be fired at it. If an arrow landed outside the circle it was called a sin. In other words it missed the mark, just like we all have when it comes to being righteous.

"As it is written, There is none righteous, no, not one."
(Romans 3:10 NIV)

The Bible makes it very clear that every one of us has sinned and that we are all in need of mercy and forgiveness from God. Without it we are all hopelessly lost and will go to a lost eternity.

"He saved us, not because of righteous things we had done, but because of his mercy". (Titus 3:5 NIV)

We deceive ourselves by saying we haven't done anything wrong:

"If we claim to be without sin, we deceive ourselves and the truth is not in us". (1 John 1:8 NIV)

But there is very good news in the Bible

"If we confess our sins, he is faithful and just and will forgive us our sins and purify us from all unrighteousness". (1 John 1:9 NIV)

I have some more great news for you. God actually took on flesh and became a human being like you and me in the person of Jesus Christ: -

"The Word became flesh and made his dwelling among us". (John 1:14 NIV)

When Jesus lived on the Earth He lived a perfectly sinless life. He asked people: - "

"Can any of you prove me guilty of sin? If I am telling the truth, why don't you believe me?" (John 8:46 NIV)

Jesus died on the Cross at Calvary in our place, taking our punishment: -

"But God demonstrates his own love for us in this: While we were still sinners, Christ died for us". (Romans 5:8 NIV)

Three days after that Jesus rose from the dead victorious over sin, death and hell.

By His Death and Resurrection and by Grace, which is receiving that which we do not deserve, we can all have our sins forgiven and have everlasting life from now into eternity; but we can only do this if we place our faith in Jesus Christ. All we have to do is believe that He died in our place and that He rose from the dead. You may recall the scripture I quoted when Desiree gave her life to Christ. It is just the same for you: -

"If you confess with your mouth that Jesus is Lord and believe in your heart that God raised Him from the dead, you will be saved." (Romans 10:9 NIV)

So it is clear that there is only one way to God and that is through His Son Jesus Christ and you can receive Him now wherever you are reading this.

Do you want to receive Jesus Christ as the Lord and follow him for the rest of your life?

If you do please read on.

Below there is a very similar prayer to the one that both Desiree and I prayed many years ago. You can read it out aloud or quietly from heart. If you genuinely mean it, God will hear it and you will be changed forever.

"Heavenly Father, I know that I am a sinner and I know that I do deserve the consequences of my sin. I ask you for forgiveness from all that I have done wrong. I want to trust in Your Son Jesus Christ to be my Saviour and I invite Him to come into my life. I believe that His death and resurrection provided for my forgiveness. I trust in Jesus and Jesus alone as my personal Lord and Saviour. Help me to follow after You and never look back. I thank you Lord, for saving me and for forgiving me. In the name of Jesus Christ. Thank you Amen!"

If you said that prayer then it has been well worth me writing this book. I am going to ask you to do five very important things:

1. TELL SOMEONE what you have done. You must verbally confess your faith in Jesus Christ. It is essential and you will soon discover that it will confirm your decision.

2. SPEAK TO GOD DAILY IN PRAYER. You don't have to speak to him in an old fashioned language in "Thees and Thous". You can talk with Him just as you would to your own earthly father. Share all your concerns and joys with Him.

3. READ THE BIBLE REGULARLY. This is very important. You will discover that the living word of God will speak to you and give you guidance.

If you have never read the Bible before, just start with the Gospel of Mark or of John in the New Testament like I did.

4. GET INVOLVED in a local Bible preaching church. You need to be around other Christians who will encourage you and help you

5. PLEASE TELL ME about your decision. You can contact me:

Via email at **gospelonetoone@gmail.com** or you can use the contact section of our website at: **www.gospelonetoone.co.uk**

You can also read my blogs, which are at **www.gospelonetoone.blogspot.com**

Or write to me at:

Gospel One to one
Unit 5812
PO Box 92
Cardiff
Wales
CF11 1NB

God   Bless   you.

Suggested reading:

Thank you very much for reading my story. If you have enjoyed learning about my journey to faith in Christ, I would like to recommend the following books to you.

The first three are very good to read if you have questions about God and the Christian faith.

'Searching Issues' by Nicky Gumbel

'Questions of life' by Nicky Gumbel

'The Life' by J.John

The last five are by people that have had gone along very different paths to me. They are all excellent in their own ways. I highly recommend them

'Taming the tiger' by Tony Anthony

'Once an addict' by Barry Woodward

'Run baby run' by Nicky Cruz

'Journey from fear to faith' by James H Summers

'Castaway Kid' by R B Mitchell

Made Simple

ONE TO ONE
WITNESSING
FOR CHRIST

- **Simple**
- **Effective**
- **Biblical**

Moray LWH McGuffie
Gospel One To One

AUTHOR OF " A FALL FROM THE TOP"

One To One Witnessing For Christ...Made Simple

The truth is that many Christians greatly fear witnessing for Christ. This is often due to them having feelings of fear or because they wish to avoid being rejected.

The content of this book gives clear, simple, effective and above all Biblical techniques that work through proven results. Filled with practical examples that clearly demonstrate how to witness, share the gospel and how to invite people to church or events. It is above all simple and easy to follow.

Moray explains that witnessing will always be easier when you make the decision to rely on the Holy Spirit to guide you as you step out in faith. In the many examples givrn you will understand that when you share your faith the Holy Spirit will always be with you.

Each of the chapters will either challenge you personally, or they will inspire you to obey the commands of Jesus when He said,"Go and preach the Gospel to all creation" Mark 16:15.

In the parable Jesus gave this example, "Then the master told his servant, 'Go out to the roads and country lanes and compel them to come in, so that my house will be full.

Luke 14: 23

Available from Amazon, Lulu and all major book sellers

Gospel One to One

This ministry has but one aim. That is the spreading of the Gospel through preaching, testifying, teaching and equipping the saints for the work of the ministry. If you are interested in Moray or Desiree speaking at your church or venue please contact us at the postal address or by going through our web site. We will do our very best to get back to you as soon as we receive your communication.

Preaching & Testifying, Teaching and Equipping the saints

Contact us via the Internet at our web site:

www.gospelonetoone.co.uk/contact

Or via email:

gospelonetoone@gmail.com

Or by mail:

Gospel One To One
Unit 5812
PO Box 92
Cardiff
Wales
CF11 1NB